P9-DER-003

j92
HAW   Henderson, Harry

            Stephen Hawking

$22.59

DATE		
DEC 2 7 1995		
SEP 2 3 1998		
SEP 2 7 2000		
MAR 2 4 2002		

Grades 7-9

01011

BAKER & TAYLOR

NOV 1 8 1995

THE IMPORTANCE OF

Stephen Hawking

by
Harry Henderson

Lucent Books, P.O. Box 289011, San Diego, CA 92198-9011

These and other titles are included in The Importance Of biography series:

Alexander the Great	Galileo Galilei	Sir Isaac Newton
Muhammad Ali	Martha Graham	Richard M. Nixon
Louis Armstrong	Stephen Hawking	Louis Pasteur
Napoleon Bonaparte	Jim Henson	Jackie Robinson
Rachel Carson	Harry Houdini	Anwar Sadat
Cleopatra	Thomas Jefferson	Margaret Sanger
Christopher Columbus	Chief Joseph	John Steinbeck
Marie Curie	Malcolm X	Jim Thorpe
Thomas Edison	Margaret Mead	Mark Twain
Albert Einstein	Michelangelo	H.G. Wells
Benjamin Franklin	Wolfgang Amadeus Mozart	

Library of Congress Cataloging-in-Publication Data

Henderson, Harry, 1951-
    Stephen Hawking / by Harry Henderson
        p. cm.—(The Importance Of)
    Includes bibliographical references and index.
    ISBN 1-56006-050-6 (acid-free paper)
    1. Hawking, S.W. (Stephen W.)—Juvenile literature. 2.
Physics—History—Juvenile literature. 3. Astrophysics—History—Juvenile literature. 4. Physicists—Great Britain—Biography—Juvenile literature. [1. Hawking, S.W. (Stephen W.) 2.
Physicists. 3. Physically handicapped. 4. Astrophysics.] I.Title.
II. Series.
QC16.H33H46   1995
530'.092—dc20
[B]   93-49488
                                                                CIP
                                                                 AC

Copyright 1995 by Lucent Books, Inc., P.O. Box 289011,
San Diego, California, 92198-9011

Printed in the U.S.A.

No part of this book may be reproduced or used in any other form or by any other means, electrical, mechanical, or otherwise, including, but not limited to photocopy, recording, or any information storage and retrieval system, without prior written permission from the publisher.

To Lisa
for bringing out the writer in me
and for so much more

Contents

Foreword

THE IMPORTANCE OF biography series deals with individuals who have made a unique contribution to history. The editors of the series have deliberately chosen to cast a wide net and include people from all fields of endeavor. Individuals from politics, music, art, literature, philosophy, science, sports, and religion are all represented. In addition, the editors did not restrict the series to individuals whose accomplishments have helped change the course of history. Of necessity, this criterion would have eliminated many whose contribution was great, though limited. Charles Darwin, for example, was responsible for radically altering the scientific view of the natural history of the world. His achievements continue to impact the study of science today. Others, such as Chief Joseph of the Nez Percé, played a pivotal role in the history of their own people. While Joseph's influence does not extend much beyond the Nez Percé, his nonviolent resistance to white expansion and his continuing role in protecting his tribe and his homeland remain an inspiration to all.

These biographies are more than factual chronicles. Each volume attempts to emphasize an individual's contributions both in his or her own time and for posterity. For example, the voyages of Christopher Columbus opened the way to European colonization of the New World. Unquestionably, his encounter with the New World brought monumental changes to both Europe and the Americas in his day. Today, however, the broader impact of Columbus's voyages is being critically scrutinized. *Christopher Columbus,* as well as every biography in The Importance Of series, includes and evaluates the most recent scholarship available on each subject.

Each author includes a wide variety of primary and secondary source quotations to document and substantiate his or her work. All quotes are footnoted to show readers exactly how and where biographers derive their information, as well as to provide stepping stones to further research. These quotations enliven the text by giving readers eyewitness views of the life and times of each individual covered in The Importance Of series.

Finally, each volume is enhanced by photographs, bibliographies, chronologies, and comprehensive indexes. For both the casual reader and the student engaged in research, The Importance Of biographies will be a fascinating adventure into the lives of people who have helped shape humanity's past and present, and who will continue to shape its future.

Important Dates in the Life of Stephen Hawking

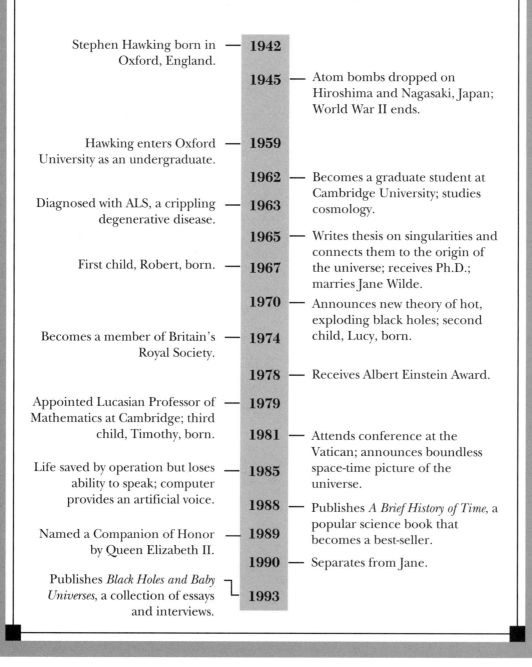

Stephen Hawking born in Oxford, England. — **1942**

1945 — Atom bombs dropped on Hiroshima and Nagasaki, Japan; World War II ends.

Hawking enters Oxford University as an undergraduate. — **1959**

1962 — Becomes a graduate student at Cambridge University; studies cosmology.

Diagnosed with ALS, a crippling degenerative disease. — **1963**

1965 — Writes thesis on singularities and connects them to the origin of the universe; receives Ph.D.; marries Jane Wilde.

First child, Robert, born. — **1967**

1970 — Announces new theory of hot, exploding black holes; second child, Lucy, born.

Becomes a member of Britain's Royal Society. — **1974**

1978 — Receives Albert Einstein Award.

Appointed Lucasian Professor of Mathematics at Cambridge; third child, Timothy, born. — **1979**

1981 — Attends conference at the Vatican; announces boundless space-time picture of the universe.

Life saved by operation but loses ability to speak; computer provides an artificial voice. — **1985**

1988 — Publishes *A Brief History of Time*, a popular science book that becomes a best-seller.

Named a Companion of Honor by Queen Elizabeth II. — **1989**

1990 — Separates from Jane.

Publishes *Black Holes and Baby Universes*, a collection of essays and interviews. — **1993**

Stephen Hawking and the Drama of Science

Many people think of science as a collection of facts and ideas about the world around us. Textbooks often describe scientific knowledge in a neat, orderly way, showing how each idea leads logically to the next. This is especially true of physics, the study of matter and energy. The seemingly unchanging laws of physics are summarized in tidy mathematical equations. Unfortunately, such neatness hides the real heart of science, the process by which human beings learn how to ask questions about the world and work out reliable and useful answers.

Intuition and Courage

The story of science is more than the unravelling of intriguing mysteries about the universe. It is also the story of how human beings have brought their individual strengths and weaknesses to the struggle to understand more about the world. Stephen Hawking is one of the best-known and most admired scientists in the world today. His life and work have been featured in numerous newspaper and magazine articles, television documentaries, and even a movie.

Afflicted with a crippling disease and using a computer to speak, British theoretical physicist Stephen Hawking ponders the secrets of the universe.

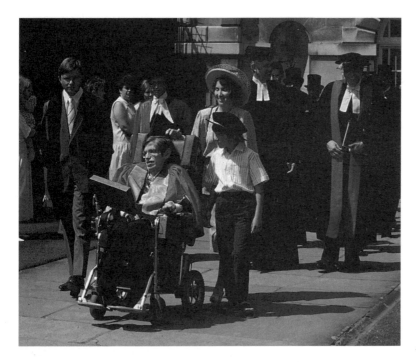

Hawking with his wife and son. Hawking—often called the most brilliant scientist since Einstein—has received numerous awards and honors for his scientific achievements.

Hawking's life story shows the personal side of science very vividly because it combines insights about the universe with a dramatic and triumphant struggle against terrible obstacles.

Part of Hawking's fame comes from his ability to use his imagination or intuition to see connections between seemingly unrelated ideas. He has combined the physical laws governing suns and galaxies with those governing the particles inside the atom. He has created a chain of thought that links events inside collapsing stars with the almost unimaginable explosion that, most scientists believe, began our universe about fifteen billion years ago.

Hawking balances his intuition with patience and discipline. These qualities are necessary for the hard, painstaking work of proving that the ideas revealed by intuition are actually true. Most good scientists possess this combination of imagination and careful attention to the details of the real world. But Stephen Hawking has been forced to develop an additional quality that sets him apart from others who might be equally talented: raw courage.

At the age of twenty-one Hawking learned that he had an incurable disease that would slowly rob him of nearly all ability to move, including even the power to speak. Drawing on a stubbornness that became legendary, he refused to give up his scientific career. Instead, he used his struggle against his disability to focus and sharpen the powers of his undamaged and brilliant mind. The result has been both excellent science and an enduring testimony to the power of the human will.

1 An Unexpected Universe

As 1942 began, Great Britain was in the third year of a bitter struggle for survival. Two years earlier the brave fliers of the Royal Air Force had beaten back Adolf Hitler's Luftwaffe, the mighty German air force, and England had been spared from invasion. But month after month, night after night, German bombers continued to pound London.

Frank and Isobel Hawking were expecting their first child. The Hawkings were well-educated and talented. They

Homeless children and rubble-strewn streets were familiar sights in London during World War II.

surrounded themselves with books and loved science and literature. Both had attended the university at Oxford. Frank Hawking was a doctor and research biologist who specialized in diseases found in warm climates. When World War II broke out in 1939, Frank was doing research in Africa. After he made his way home, the government decided that he was more valuable as a researcher in England than on the front lines, so he did not have to join the armed forces.

Isobel met Frank Hawking while she was working as a secretary at a medical research institute. She was the daughter of a doctor in Glasgow, Scotland. In the early twentieth century most people in Great Britain didn't think it was important for a woman to go to college. Isobel's parents disagreed, and they had made sacrifices to pay for their daughter's schooling.

A Safe Haven

Thinking about their family's future in those dark days was hard enough, but almost every night brought the couple something more immediate to worry about. Like other Londoners, the Hawkings would hear the bombers roaring overhead. No one knew where a bomb would land next. Many Londoners, however, developed an almost casual attitude to hide their fear. As Isobel Hawking recalls, "when you heard the bang, you knew it wasn't you, so you went back to your meal or whatever."[1]

One night one bomb fell so close to the Hawkings' home that the explosion blew in their back windows. The Hawkings decided at that moment that they would leave battered London and go to Oxford, a famous

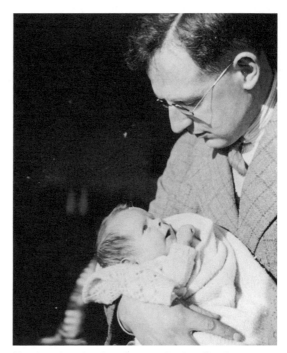

Fearing the relentless German Luftwaffe, the Hawkings left London and moved to Oxford where Stephen was born. Here, Frank Hawking holds newborn Stephen.

university town, for their first child's birth. Stephen Hawking noted later that

> Oxford was a good place to be born during the war: the Germans had an agreement that they would not bomb Oxford and Cambridge, in return for the British not bombing Heidelberg and Göttingen. It is a pity that this civilized sort of arrangement couldn't have been extended to more areas.[2]

The Expanding Universe of Science

Stephen Hawking once noted that he "was born on January the 8th, 1942, exactly three hundred years after the death of Galileo."[3] It is not surprising that someone who would contribute so much to the understanding of the universe as Hawking should point out this coincidence. Galileo had completely changed people's view of the universe by proving the idea of another thinker, Copernicus, that the earth was one of a family of planets circling the sun. Before Galileo's time most people had believed that the earth was the center of the universe. By the early twentieth century astronomers with ever more powerful telescopes had discovered that our sun was just one of millions of stars in a galaxy called the Milky Way, which in turn was adrift in a sea of millions of other galaxies that were separated by almost unimaginable distances.

In the early twentieth century, Einstein's theories profoundly changed the way people thought about the world.

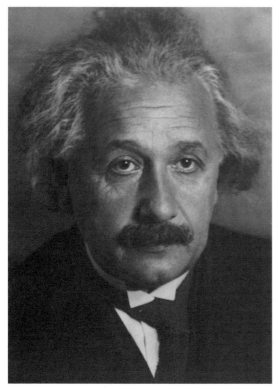

Science had changed just as greatly in the decades before Stephen Hawking's birth. Albert Einstein had introduced his theories of relativity with their surprising conclusions about curved space-time and the strange behavior of objects moving close to the speed of light. Physicists had taken their first looks inside the tiny world of the atom.

The theories of Einstein and the discoveries of modern astronomy, together with the new biology pioneered by Darwin in the nineteenth century, had profoundly changed the way people thought about themselves and the world. The universe, it seemed, was much bigger and much older than anyone had imagined. These theoretical discoveries seemed to have little to do with everyday life, however.

But World War II changed the way people looked at scientists and their theories. Suddenly the abstruse, or incomprehensible, ideas of physics had become very important indeed. The laws of gravity and motion, discovered centuries earlier by Newton, now enabled warring nations to aim and launch rocket bombs that flew hundreds of miles, scraping the edge of space before plunging down on their targets. Newton's law of action and reaction propelled both rockets and new jet airplanes that would soon break the sound barrier.

The invisible world inside the atom, too, became a key to practical technology. The ability to harness the flow of electrons brought forth radar, television, and the computer. Scientists had learned to split atoms apart. Einstein's famous equation, $E=mc^2$, showing how matter could be turned into energy, had led to the terrible

reality of the atom bombs bursting over Hiroshima and Nagasaki in Japan in 1945.

After World War II ended it became clear that the nations that could most effectively harness science and technology would gain the upper hand in the new cold war between Western and Soviet countries. Physicists in particular were in great demand. Science became a more important part of the school curriculum, especially after the Soviets launched *Sputnik*, the first artificial earth satellite, in 1957. Children of Hawking's generation had a greater opportunity than ever before to be exposed to the exciting and swiftly changing world of science.

The advent of the atom bomb revealed the enormous consequences of the practical application of nuclear science. When the bomb was unleashed over Hiroshima and Nagasaki in 1945, the scope of destruction was unprecedented (right). Hawking's generation, too, was exposed to the swiftly changing world of science. In 1957, for example, the Soviets launched the world's first artificial satellite, Sputnik (above).

School Days, Games, and Gadgets

What family and friends first noticed about Stephen Hawking was his lively imagination. When little Stephen made up an imaginary house, it was so real to him that, while out walking with his mother, he would try and board a passing bus that he thought could take him there. Stephen talked so rapidly that his mind seemed to race ahead of his words, sometimes making him stutter.

In 1950 the Hawkings moved to St. Albans, an ancient and prosperous town. Stephen's father decided to send his eight-year-old son to a private school. Many wealthy and middle-class English families sent their children to private schools because they believed that such schooling gave their children an advantage over public school graduates.

Frank Hawking wanted Stephen to go to Westminster School, one of the most exclusive—and expensive—of British private schools. The Hawkings could not afford the high fees charged by this school, so Stephen had to take an examination in the hope of winning a scholarship. Unfortunately, Stephen fell ill on exam day and lost his chance. He entered a private school in St. Albans in 1952.

Stephen did well in school, though he was not at the top of his class. By age fifteen, however, he was part of the "smart set" of teenage students who listened to classical music, argued about literature and philosophy, and solved physics problems.

During holidays Stephen designed elaborate games for his friends. One was a war game that recreated all of World War II. An even more elaborate game, called the Feudal Game, was based on England in the Middle Ages. With its many maps

An early photo of Hawking and his siblings. Even as a child, Hawking exhibited a lively imagination.

The young Hawking poses with his new bicycle (left) and at the helm (below).

and charts, it was at least as complicated as the dungeon games that teenagers would be playing twenty-five years later. Michael Church, Stephen's fellow gamer, recalls that Stephen "loved the fact that he had created the [game] world and then created the laws that governed it. And that he was causing us to obey those laws: he enjoyed that, too."[4] Hawking's pleasure in creating the laws for an imaginary world would later be transformed into an equally great pleasure in discovering the laws that had caused the real universe to come into being.

While he was still a teenager, Stephen and some of his mathematically inclined friends decided to build a computer. This seemed like a ridiculous notion, since the computers that existed in the late 1950s were room-sized collections of vacuum tubes that cost hundreds of thousands of dollars and sat in big universities, corporations, and government offices. Stephen and his friends nonetheless gathered an assortment of telephone switches, relays, and other parts and managed to build a working computer that could solve complicated logic problems. The machine was so amazing that it was written up in the local newspaper.

Much as Stephen loved building model airplanes, computers, and other electronic gadgetry, it became clear that he was not very skilled at putting things together with his hands. His brilliance lay in creating systems and testing theories, putting ideas together in his mind. As Stephen began to study advanced mathematics and science, his high test scores and work began to attract notice.

Fierce Competition

As Stephen began his last year at St. Albans, he had to make some decisions about college. Stephen's father, being an Oxford graduate, naturally wanted his son to go to that university. Competition for places at Oxford was fierce, however. Hawking's father tried to pull some strings to help his son's chances, but the most important hurdle was one that Stephen would have to jump by himself: the entrance exams. There was a series of them, spread over two days. The tests emphasized math and physics, but Stephen also had to answer essay questions about general knowledge and world affairs.

After the written tests came the orals, which were even more intimidating. A panel of officials and professors fired questions at each nervous student. They often made the questions hard and tricky on purpose, to see if the student could stand up under pressure. After his orals Stephen was interviewed in detail about his knowledge of physics, the subject in which he had decided to specialize.

After ten days of anxious waiting Stephen received an invitation for a further interview at Oxford. This meant that he had made the first cut and had a decent chance of being accepted. (In fact, he had scored around 95 percent on his examination papers.) Shortly after the second interview Stephen got a letter of acceptance to Oxford.

Oxford and the Exciting Sixties

Oxford University is more like a small, sprawling city than an ordinary college campus. Founded in the 1100s, Oxford grew over the centuries into a federation of thirty-five separate, self-governing colleges. Most of the colleges are built around quads (quadrangles, or rectangular open spaces). Paths meander around the quads. Buildings from the Middle Ages bump up against modern office buildings and laboratories. For Stephen Hawking, a graduate of a small private school like St. Albans, the world of Oxford was bound to take some getting used to.

In 1959, when Hawking entered Oxford, the university's students were still mainly upper-class and male. The wealthier students had their own servants, called scouts, who cleaned their rooms and awakened them in time for breakfast. The students who came from upper-class families saw themselves as privileged and special. They didn't mix very much with other students such as Stephen Hawking, who had come from middle-class or working-class families. Life at Oxford was starting to change at this time, however. Some students began to rebel against the university's traditions. They listened to new kinds of poetry and music. Many became involved in politics. As he looked for a way to fit into university life, Stephen found that he had many different role models to choose from.

In fact, this seemingly new desire for freedom fitted in very well with Oxford's traditions. The university expected students to work in an independent fashion. Instead of taking regularly scheduled classes and tests, each student was assigned a personal tutor who guided his or her studies. Students attended lectures and had weekly tutorials, or meetings with their tutors, to discuss problems. Only the tests at the end of the first and final years counted toward a degree. In this relaxed atmosphere, Hawking had a hard time applying himself to regular study.

Oxford in the 1950s. Hawking entered the university in 1959, and soon realized he could get by without exerting himself academically. Indeed, he worked just hard enough to reveal a brilliant intellect.

Sitting at the stern, a carefree Hawking commands a crew of eight rowers. As coxswain of the rowing team, Hawking spent many happy afternoons on the river.

During his undergraduate years at Oxford, developing a more rounded social life was more important to Hawking than studying. He quickly became involved in rowing, a sport popular with fashionable Oxford students. Even though Stephen wasn't big or strong enough to handle an oar, he did find a place on the crew. Each crew had eight rowers and a coxswain, or steerer. The cox sat in the stern of the boat, yelling out the commands that controlled the rhythm and direction of the rowing. Stephen became a good, if not first-class, cox. His interest in rowing helped relieve some of the boredom he felt in his physics studies, which didn't seem much more advanced than what he had already done at St. Albans. Perhaps more importantly, rowing made Stephen part of a team and gave him a sense of belonging. On a typical day, Stephen raced through his physics experiments, collecting just enough data to get by, and then spent the afternoon on the river.

Graduation

After nearly three years had passed, it was time for finals. These examinations would determine how high a degree Stephen would get. (A first-class degree was best, while a fourth-class degree meant barely getting by.) Hawking later calculated that he had studied an average of only an hour a day during his three years at Oxford. Now, with finals approaching, a friend remarked with amusement that "towards the end he was working as much as three hours a day."[5]

But Stephen had a plan to beat the tests. He would use his quick grasp of theory to make up for his lack of preparation.

> Because of my lack of work, I had planned to get through the final exam by doing problems in theoretical physics and avoiding any questions that required factual knowledge. I didn't do very well. I was on the borderline between a first- and second-class degree.[6]

An Oxford street scene during Stephen's term at the university.

Stephen wanted to go to graduate school at Cambridge, another large and famous British university. To be accepted he would have to pass his finals with the highest possible honors. Since his test scores were borderline, his final degree would depend on a personal interview with the examiners.

The interview went well, because Hawking's tutor and other teachers were impressed with his ability. They thought Stephen would settle down and do fine work in physics. The examiners admired Hawking's dry wit. When the chief examiner asked him what his career plans were, Hawking answered, "If you award me a First [class degree], I will go to Cambridge. If I receive a Second, I shall stay in Oxford, so I expect you will give me a First."[7] Hawking got his First and entered Cambridge in 1962.

Cambridge and Cosmology

Stephen Hawking found graduate work at Cambridge much tougher than studying at Oxford had been. He learned that he had to struggle against his casual attitude toward work and begin studying regularly. He also had to decide what subject he was going to research for his doctoral degree.

Broadly speaking, Hawking had two choices if he pursued physics: elementary particles and cosmology. Elementary particles were the mysterious particles inside the atom. Hawking recalls:

> I thought that elementary particles were less attractive, because, although they were finding lots of new particles,

A Reckless Rower

In their biography of Hawking, authors Michael White and John Gribbin describe how Norman Dix, Hawking's rowing coach, remembers Stephen's carefree but exuberant attitude toward the sport:

"Dix remembers Hawking as a boisterous young fellow who from the beginning cultivated a daredevil image when it came to navigating his crew on the river. Many was the time he would return the eight [rowers] to shore with bits of the boat knocked off and oar blades damaged, because he tried to guide his crew through an impossibly narrow gap and had come to grief. Dix never did believe Hawking's claim that 'something had got in the way.' 'Half the time,' says Dix, 'I got the distinct impression that he was sitting in the stern of the boat with his head in the stars, working out his mathematical formula[s].' "

there was no proper theory of elementary particles. All they could do was arrange the particles in families, like in botany [the study of plants].[8]

Cosmology, the study of the nature and origin of the universe, appealed to Hawking more. It focused on some fascinating questions about which new theories could be applied. How big was the universe? Why was it growing bigger all the time? How did the universe begin? Would the universe die someday or go on existing forever? Hawking quickly decided that cosmology was the field of physics that he would pursue.

Steady State or Big Bang?

By the time Stephen Hawking was getting ready to take up cosmology, scientists had worked out two main theories about the origin of the universe. One, the "steady state" theory, was associated with Fred Hoyle, a famous astronomer whom Hawking would soon meet at Cambridge. According to Hoyle, the universe was something like a huge balloon with stars painted on its surface. As space expanded (or the balloon was blown up), galaxies (or the stars) grew farther apart. Since galaxies seemed to be distributed evenly throughout the known universe, Hoyle theorized that new stars and galaxies were constantly created to fill in the spaces that appeared as galaxies moved farther apart. Hoyle concluded that the universe grew smoothly and steadily.

But new observations began to contradict the steady state theory. Light and other forms of radiation, including radio waves, travel at a fixed speed. Saying, for example, that a star is one hundred light-years away means that it takes light one hundred years to travel from that star to an observer on earth. Thus the farther away a source of light or radio waves is from us, the longer ago the radiation we detect must have left the source. (Light from a star five hundred light-years away picked up in today's telescopes began its journey at the time Columbus was first telling Europeans about the lands he had found.)

After World War II astronomers had built radio telescopes that could see even farther into space than light-gathering telescopes. The radio waves they were picking up on their receivers started their journey millions or even billions of years ago. Studying these distant objects is like getting a snapshot of what the universe looked like at the time the light or radio waves began their journey. By looking at the spectrum, or arrangement of the light or radio waves, astronomers began to learn more about the physical conditions of the early universe. They also made a remarkable discovery: they found that the whole universe seems to be filled with a faint but detectable background radiation.

Some cosmologists theorized that this radiation was left over from a huge explosion, or Big Bang, that had created the universe. As the radiation spread outward

Radio telescopes enabled scientists to learn more about the conditions of the early universe.

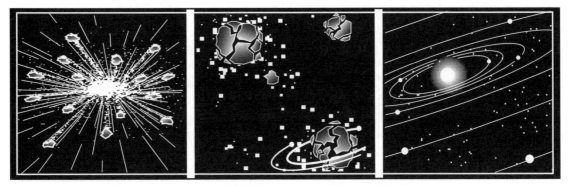

Many scientists theorize that all the matter that is now the universe once existed in a small, dense space. An explosion, known as the Big Bang, hurtled the matter through space (left). Gradually, gravity attracted the masses together, forming stars and planets (middle). Over time, some planets were drawn into orbits around stars, and likewise, moons around planets (right). Similarly, entire solar systems revolve around galaxies.

from the explosion, it gradually cooled and began to be replaced by matter—stars and galaxies. (Einstein's famous equation, $E=mc^2$, means that energy can change to matter, and the reverse, under the right conditions.)

When Stars Die

Besides the question of the origin of the universe, cosmology also offered young Hawking another puzzle. What happens to stars when they die? By the 1930s astronomers had learned that stars eventually ran out of the hydrogen gas that fuels their atomic "furnaces." As a star's light energy diminishes, the outer layers of the star begin to be pulled inward by the star's gravity. The star starts to collapse. Some stars eventually turn into small, dense, so-called white dwarfs that pack a sun's worth of material into a space about the size of the earth. An India-born astronomer named Subrahmanyan Chandrasekhar

found in the late 1930s that not all stars became white dwarfs. If a star was about 1.4 times or more massive than the sun, the electrons in the collapsing gases began to move at close to light speed. At this speed, Einstein's relativity equations came into play and stopped the star from settling down as a white dwarf. Would these larger stars shrink forever, disappear, or perhaps explode? No one knew for sure, but applying relativity theory to the inside of stars might lead to a cosmic breakthrough.

A Shadow Falls

Hawking had hoped to study with the famous Fred Hoyle, but for his tutor he got a much less well-known cosmologist named Dennis Sciama. Although Hawking was disappointed, he soon found that Sciama was both a fine scientist and a helpful mentor who always had time for his students. Hoyle, who was often traveling around the world, would actually have been far less instrumental in Hawking's development as a scientist.

In his first term at Cambridge Hawking struggled to master the extremely complex mathematics needed to understand Albert Einstein's theory of relativity. Hawking knew that he would have to have a good grasp of this theory before he could investigate any cosmological problem. He also needed to find a suitable research topic for the long paper, or thesis, that he would need to complete to obtain his advanced degree. He was working near the frontiers of cosmology, and it was hard to find a topic that was both interesting and manageable. Looking back, Sciama thinks that Hawking came close to losing his way and even flunking out of school at this time. Hawking seemed to need some outside force to make him focus on his goal.

When that force came, it was a devastating one. For some time Stephen had begun to notice that he was getting clumsier. His hands didn't seem to work quite right. He often spilled a drink that he was trying to pour, and he tended to fall down unexpectedly. When Stephen came home after his first term at Cambridge, his parents noticed the problem as well. They thought it might have been caused by a disease that he had picked up during a trip to Persia (Iran) the previous summer. But they sent Stephen to their family doctor, who in turn sent him to a specialist.

Hawking recalls:

> Shortly after my twenty-first birthday, I went into the hospital for tests. They took a muscle sample from my arm, stuck electrodes into me, and injected some radio-opaque fluid into my spine, and watched it going up and down with X rays as they tilted the bed. I was diagnosed as having ALS, amyotrophic lateral sclerosis, or motor neurone disease, as it is known in England.
>
> The realization that I had an incurable disease that was likely to kill me in a few years was a bit of a shock. How could something like that happen to me?[9]

Understandably, finding he had ALS was more than "a bit of shock" for Stephen. He became very depressed. He told a friend that

> he was gradually going to lose the use of his body. And that they'd told him eventually he would essentially have

Dennis Sciama, Hawking's tutor at Cambridge. Although Sciama was not his first choice, Hawking found the cosmologist capable and helpful.

A Different Planet

In A Reader's Companion *Derek Powney, one of Hawking's fellow students, recalls an incident that showed how little trouble Stephen had with his class work:*

"We were asked to read a chapter, chapter ten, in a book called *Electricity and Magnetism*. . . . At the end of the chapter there were thirteen questions, and all of them were final honors questions. Our tutor, Bobby Berman, said, 'Do as many as you can.'

So we had a go and I discovered very rapidly that I couldn't do any of them. Richard was my partner, and we worked together for the week and managed to do one and a half questions, of which we felt very proud. Gordon refused all assistance and managed to do one by himself. Stephen, as always, hadn't started.

'Ah, Hawking!' I said [around noon on the last day]. 'How many have you managed to do, then?'

'Well,' he said, 'I've only had time to do the first ten.' We fell about with laughter, which just froze on our lips because he was looking at us very quizzically. We suddenly realized that that's exactly what he had done—the first ten. I think at that point we realized that it was not just that we weren't in the same street [as Stephen], we weren't on the same planet."

the body of a cabbage but his mind would still be in perfect working order, and he would be unable to communicate with the rest of the world. He said that at the end only his heart and his lungs and his mind would still be working. After that, either his heart or lungs would give up. Then he would die.[10]

But something new was about to come into the equation of Stephen Hawking's life.

2 Journey into Darkness

As one might expect, the news that he had a crippling, incurable disease shocked Stephen Hawking. Shock soon gave way to a deep depression. Hawking shut himself away in his room for hours, listening to the mournful music of the German composer Wagner, which spoke of death, destruction, and the end of the world. Later Hawking would say that reports that he drank heavily during that time were exaggerated. But there is no doubt that his life was brought to an almost complete standstill for a while.

Learning to Live Again

Fortunately, certain experiences began to lead Hawking away from self-pity. He recalls:

> While I had been in hospital, I had seen a boy I vaguely knew die of leukemia [a kind of blood cancer], in the bed opposite me. It had not been a pretty sight. Clearly there were people who were worse off than me. At least my condition didn't make me feel sick. Whenever I feel inclined to be sorry for myself, I remember that boy.[11]

Hawking also had two dreams that made a great impression on him.

> My dreams at that time were rather disturbed. Before my condition had been diagnosed I had been very bored with life. There had not seemed to be anything worth doing. But shortly after I came out of hospital, I dreamed that I was going to be executed. I suddenly realized that there were a lot of worthwhile things I could do if I were reprieved [allowed to live].
>
> One result of my illness: when one is faced with the possibility of an early death, it makes one realize that life is worth living.[12]

In another dream Hawking felt that he could sacrifice his life to help others: "After all, if I were going to die anyway, it might as well do some good," he heard his dreaming self say.[13]

These feelings and dreams helped Hawking put things in better perspective. What really restored his will to live, however, was his growing friendship with Jane Wilde. Jane was a student of modern languages whom Hawking had talked to for a long time at a party on New Year's Day, 1963. Jane had quickly been drawn to the brilliant if somewhat eccentric young man. She seemed to sense both his great potential and the difficulties to come. As she recalled later, "There was something lost. He knew something was happening to him of which he wasn't in control."[14] Stephen, in turn, was attracted to Jane's energetic, outgoing personality. They fell deeply in love and soon were engaged to be married.

"The engagement changed my life," Hawking recalls. "It gave me something to live for. It made me determined to live. Without the help that Jane has given I would not have been able to carry on, nor have had the will to do so."[15]

ALS is an unpredictable disease. While a person with ALS never gets better, the disease will often stop progressing for a time, sometimes for many years. Despite the doctors' prediction that he had less than two years to live, Hawking's condition began to stabilize. Although he now needed a walking stick to get around, gradually it became clear that Hawking had been granted the reprieve he had sought in his dream. It was time to get back to work.

Cambridge and Physics

Hawking began his graduate study at the Department of Applied Mathematics and Theoretical Physics (DAMTP) at Cambridge University. His past lazy work habits began to vanish. Not only did Hawking now realize that each year was precious, but he also had an urgent and practical reason to work hard. In order to get married, he had to have a job that could support a future family. To get a job as a scientist, he first needed a Ph.D., or doctoral degree. The main requirement for the de-

gree was writing a thesis, or long paper that described a piece of original research that could stand up to close examination.

Hawking also responded to the stimulating presence of his advisor, Dennis Sciama, and of his fellow graduate students, some of whom soon became good friends. The working environment at DAMTP was ideal for encouraging the sharing of ideas and insights. Sciama gave Hawking and his other thesis students pointers and encouragement but otherwise left them free to explore new ideas, even ones that seemed to be outrageous. Sciama and his students darted in and out of each other's offices, brainstorming one idea after another. The whole group met each morning for coffee and in the afternoon for tea. In the buzz of conversation the latest ideas and speculations made their way around the room so that everyone knew what everyone else was working on.

A Dramatic Confrontation

By the early 1960s Fred Hoyle had become one of the world's leading astrophysicists—scientists who study the physical processes that take place within stars and galaxies. Energetic and outgoing, he had a flair for popularizing his theories about the structure of the universe. He traveled widely, giving lectures to raise money for his research.

Fred Hoyle had given Jayant Narlikar, one of Hawking's fellow students, the task of working out the mathematics to support Hoyle's new steady-state theories. Hawking, looking for interesting cosmological problems, became interested in Narlikar's equations. Soon Hawking and

Narlikar were spending hours going over the math together.

One afternoon in 1963 Hoyle gave a talk at the Royal Society in London, one of the world's foremost scientific organizations. Hoyle was presenting new evidence for his theory that the universe existed in a steady state without beginning or end. To Hoyle this theory was much more sensible than the alternative theory, which he later ridiculed by giving the name Big Bang. The latter, he said, was something like a party girl jumping out of a birthday cake.

How could a universe suddenly come out of nothing? Hoyle was so confident about the correctness of his new work that he had skipped the usual step of having his work reviewed by other scientists.

Hoyle's talk was met with considerable applause. He then asked if there were any questions. A young man, looking frail but intense, leaned awkwardly on his walking stick as he stood up. "The quantity you're talking about diverges," he said. This meant that the mathematics actually disproved, rather than proved, Hoyle's new

An aerial view of Cambridge University, where Hawking pursued his doctoral degree.

A Singular Idea

Despite the dramatic way he had introduced himself to the world of physics, Hawking still needed to find a topic in cosmology that he could use for his own thesis. Hawking and the other students in Sciama's research group had begun to meet with Roger Penrose, a mathematician who was working with a fascinating concept called a singularity.

To get an idea of what a singularity is like, imagine that you are infinitely strong—even stronger than Arnold Schwarzenegger or the mightiest comic book superhero. You crush a beach ball with your hands until it is smaller than a basketball—then smaller than a baseball, smaller than a marble, smaller than you can see . . . smaller and smaller. As you crush the ball, it gets denser and denser, since the same amount of matter is being forced into a smaller and smaller space. Eventually even the atoms and the particles that make up the atoms are crushed. You reach a point where the object is infinitely dense and infinitely small. This is the singularity.

Black Holes

Hawking became fascinated by the idea of singularity. Furthermore, although singularities seemed at first to be terribly abstract and without relevance to the real universe, astronomers in the 1960s were beginning to find evidence that singularities might be at the heart of mysterious objects that were showing up at the limits of their instruments' range.

Fred Hoyle was one of the world's leading astrophysicists during the 1960s. In 1963, Hawking attended Hoyle's lecture at the Royal Society. Undaunted by Hoyle's fame, the young, unknown Hawking rose from the audience and challenged Hoyle's theories.

theory. "Of course it doesn't diverge," Hoyle said. The young man answered just as insistently: "It does." The audience had quieted, watching the debate unfold. Hoyle, sounding quite exasperated, barked out in his formidable voice, "How do you know?" "Because I worked it out," the young man said slowly.[16]

Hoyle was furious at the bombshell that had been dropped on him by a young, unknown physics student named Stephen Hawking. But Hawking turned out to be right, and Hoyle soon calmed down, recognizing the quality of Hawking's work. Soon the world of astronomy and physics would be hearing a lot more from Stephen Hawking.

In 1969, physicist John Wheeler of Princeton dubbed a singularity a "black hole."

Chandrasekhar had shown in the 1930s that if an exhausted, collapsing star were big enough, it would not settle down into a dense but stable ministar called a white dwarf as smaller stars do. Since that time some astronomers had speculated that larger collapsing stars might shrink forever, getting smaller and denser. Eventually, when it was only a few miles across, such a star might become so dense that it contained a singularity. It would become what physicist John Wheeler would in 1969 call a black hole.

As a physical body, a singularity or black hole was expected to have some very strange properties. A black hole would still have most of the mass that it had when it was a full-sized star, but its surface would now be very close to the body's center of mass. As a result, the force of gravity at the surface would be immense—so powerful, in fact, that anything that entered the black hole would be trapped inside, and

---

Indirect Evidence of Black Holes

In A Reader's Companion *physicist John Wheeler uses an analogy to explain how a black hole, while itself invisible, might be detected through its influence on a nearby body:*

"Friends ask me, 'What if a black hole is black? How can you see it?' And I say, have you ever been to a ball? Have you ever watched the young men dressed in their black evening tuxedos and the girls in their white dresses whirling around, held in each others' arms, and the lights turned low? And all you can see is the girls. Well, the girl is the ordinary star and the boy is the black hole. You can't see the black hole any more than you can see the boy. But the girl going around gives you convincing evidence that there must be something there holding her in orbit."

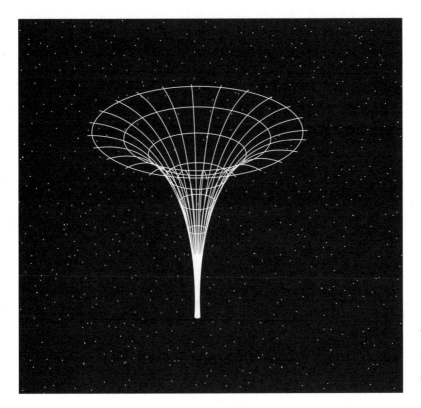

Because of its extreme density, the gravity well of a black hole is very deep. No one really knows what the inside of a black hole is like.

nothing, not even light, could ever come out. Put another way, a black hole would bend space so completely around itself that it would, in effect, disappear into a private universe of its own.

Astronomers before the 1960s tended to regard black holes as being of no more than theoretical interest. After all, assuming a black hole actually existed, how could you find it? It wouldn't give out any light or radio waves, and, being so small, a black hole couldn't block out the light of another object, such as a star, and be detected like a planet coming between the earth and sun.

By 1963, however, astronomers using radio telescopes had found very powerful radio stars. These starlike objects, it turned out, weren't nearby stars in our own galaxy. On the contrary, they were very far away. (Today most astronomers believe that they are the most distant known objects, as far as twelve billion light years away.) Astronomers began calling these objects quasars, meaning quasi-stellar (starlike) radio sources.

Astronomers soon realized that in order for an object so far away to send out such powerful radio waves, it had to be generating an incredible amount of energy—giving a brightness equivalent to about three hundred billion times that of our sun! Where could all that energy be coming from? According to Einstein's famous equation, $E=mc^2$, a relatively small amount of matter is equivalent to a great deal of energy. Quasars have about one hundred million times the mass of our sun. Somehow they were converting large amounts of matter into incredible amounts of energy—much more than could be accounted for by the nuclear fusion process that powers ordinary stars.

Gradually many astronomers came to believe that a quasar was in fact a black hole in which matter representing the center of a whole galaxy was crushed together into a space about the size of our solar system. The quasar's energy was generated as large amounts of matter were sucked into the black hole and torn apart by the tug of its intense gravity.

The discovery of quasars, and a few years later, that of dense, spinning stars called pulsars, suggested that dense bodies and even singularities might be the key to understanding the past and future of our universe. Conditions in a quasar might be similar to those found in the original Big Bang that was believed to have created the universe. As the second part of the 1960s began, the Big Bang theory triumphed over Hoyle's Steady State theory as a basic description of the way the universe was formed. One key piece of new evidence supporting the Big Bang was the discovery of faint microwave radiation that seemed to fill all of space uniformly. The uniformity meant that it must have come from a single great explosion, spreading outward something like ripples in a pond.

Another piece of evidence supporting the Big Bang came, ironically, from its chief opponent, Fred Hoyle. Hoyle and his colleagues showed how all the chemical elements that make up stars, rocks, trees, and people could have been built up from the original hydrogen and helium inside stars. The new findings also predicted the background radiation the astronomers later detected, neatly tying together support for the Big Bang.

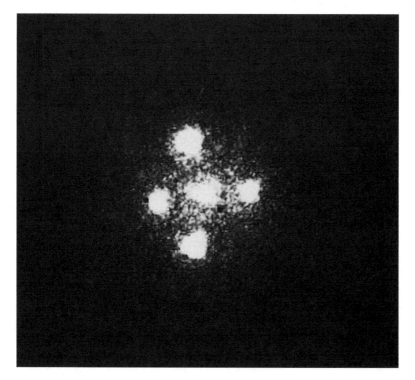

Quasars, which have been detected in the farthest reaches of the universe, radiate massive amounts of energy into space. Many astronomers think quasars are, in fact, black holes.

A Friendly Bet

One likely candidate for a black hole is a star system called Cygnus X-1, where a star seems to be in the process of being pulled apart by the gravity of an unseen companion. In A Brief History of Time *Hawking gives his opinion on the matter . . . but hedges it with a bet:*

"The best explanation for this phenomenon is that matter has been blown off the surface of the visible star. As it falls toward the unseen companion, it develops a spiral motion (rather like water running out of a bath), and it gets very hot, emitting X rays. For this mechanism to work, the unseen object has to be very small, like a white dwarf, neutron star, or black hole. From the observed orbit of the visible star, one can determine the lowest possible mass of the unseen object. In the case of Cygnus X-1, this is about six times the mass of the sun, which, according to Chandrasekhar's result, is too great . . . to be a white dwarf. It is also too large a mass to be a neutron star. It seems, therefore, that it must be a black hole. . . .

Despite this, I have a bet with Kip Thorne of the California Institute of Technology that in fact Cygnus X-1 does not contain a black hole! This is a form of insurance policy for me. I have done a lot of work on black holes, and it would all be wasted if it turned out that black holes did not exist. But in that case, I would have the consolation of winning my bet, which would bring me four years of the magazine *Private Eye*. If black holes do exist, Kip will get one year of *Penthouse*."

An artist's conception of Cygnus X-1, showing the star's matter spiraling into a black hole.

Thus by the mid-1960s both singularities and the Big Bang had become hot topics in cosmology. Stephen Hawking, with his intense interest in the special conditions of singularities, found himself at center stage in the unveiling of a new Big Bang cosmology. Along with other cosmologists, he struggled to answer the question of how the Big Bang had resulted in the immense, expanding, and largely uniform universe that we see today.

A Black Hole in Reverse

Roger Penrose and Stephen Hawking worked well together: Penrose was a master mathematician, whereas abstract mathematics had always been one of Hawking's weak areas. Hawking, on the other hand, had a powerful, intuitive way of visualizing physical problems. Their strengths complemented each other.

Mathematician Roger Penrose (left) first theorized that when a star collapses, it is crushed to a point of infinite density. Hawking imagined that if time ran backwards, this singularity would explode outward, looking something like the Big Bang.

One evening Hawking, Sciama, and other colleagues were sitting in a train compartment discussing one of their singularity meetings. Hawking's mind drifted away from the discussion, which had become stuck on a tiny technical point. Suddenly, Hawking turned to Sciama and said: "I wonder what would happen if you applied Roger's singularity theory to the entire universe."[17] What might that mean?

Let's say you are watching a movie animation of a black hole. You see matter collapsing into an infinitely dense point, the singularity. But what happens if you run the film backwards? You will see an infinitely dense point that appears to explode outward. This explosion outward from nothing is exactly what the Big Bang looks like!

By applying Penrose's singularity theory to the origin of the universe, Hawking had found the start of his life's work. He had also at last found a suitable thesis topic. Hawking set to work and found that he was enjoying himself. "I . . . started working hard for the first time in my life. To my surprise, I found I liked it. Maybe it is not really fair to call it work."[18]

Hawking's thesis was of uneven quality, reflecting the uncertainty of his earlier work. But the final chapter, which applied singularity theory to the origin of the universe, impressed the examiners as brilliant. Hawking's thesis summed up the future direction of his work with these words: "There is a singularity in our past."[19] In his thesis and in work done during the following few years, Hawking showed that if you assume that the universe is uniform and looks about the same everywhere, Einstein's relativity equations lead it back to a singularity at the beginning of time. Hawking would spend the next twenty years and more unraveling the mysteries of that singularity.

In 1965, Hawking received his Ph.D. and could now call himself Doctor Stephen Hawking. Stephen and Jane were married in July of that year—an occasion that must have felt both festive and triumphant.

3 Inside a Black Hole

In the decade following his graduation Stephen Hawking would face three kinds of challenges. The first challenge was establishing a career: getting a position that could provide financial support for him and his family and learning how to work as a scientist in an exacting field. The second challenge was scientific: the puzzling nature of black holes would pose difficult questions that would require Hawking to change his approach to physics. The third challenge was one that few of Hawking's fellow scientists would ever have to face: coping with a crippling disease that could only get worse.

The Hawkings' wedding was followed by a one-week honeymoon in the English countryside. As soon as they got back, Stephen and Jane packed their bags to travel to the United States, where Stephen attended a summer class in general relativity at Cornell University in New York. (General relativity is the theory first developed by Albert Einstein that relates space and time to gravity.)

The experience was quite valuable for Stephen but proved less happy for Jane. Stephen recalls: "It put quite a strain on our marriage, especially as we stayed in a dormitory that was full of couples with noisy small children. However, the summer school was very useful for me because

I met many of the leading people in the field."[20]

In some ways this experience set the pattern of their life to come. The work of a top ranking physicist involves a great deal of travel to conferences and seminars around the world. Over the years the constant moving about and disruption, the growing necessity to care for Stephen's every physical need, and the raising of three children would make it hard for Jane to pursue her own academic career. It would frustrate her and eventually weaken their marriage.

During the year preceding his graduation and marriage, Hawking had begun to prepare for the next stage of his career. As at most academic institutions, the colleges that make up Cambridge University offer a limited number of fellowships to the best, most promising researchers in each field. A fellowship usually provides a grant of money that supports the researcher. In exchange, the university hopes to benefit from the scientific breakthroughs the researcher may make. Hawking applied for and received a fellowship at Caius (pronounced *keys*) College at Cambridge.

Upon returning to Cambridge from their trip to America, the Hawkings had the problem of finding suitable housing. Although he was a Caius fellow, Stephen

Life at the DAMTP

In Lonely Hearts of the Cosmos *Dennis Overbye describes what he saw on a visit to Hawking's office in the 1970s:*

"There was a Black Holes Are Out of Sight bumper sticker on the door of Hawking's office at the Department of Applied Mathematics and Theoretical Physics, a grimy, industrial-looking brick building off a narrow side street. The office inside was long and narrow, with a shiny concrete floor and a stage for maneuvering a wheelchair, surrounded by an automatic page-turner, a knob-activated computer, other mechanical aids, and dusty packed bookshelves. On every vertical surface papers were taped up and books were propped open so that Hawking could look at them. . . .

I had arrived at eleven, just in time for morning tea. Like Sciama before him, Hawking had gathered a crop of graduate students around himself. In age, dress, pallor, and evidence of nutritional deficiency, they resembled the road crew for a rock and roll band. I found them gathered around a white Formica table off a hallway, cracking jokes and scribbling equations on the tabletop. . . . The tabletop, I noticed, was veined with faint blue writing and mathematics, testimony to last year's hot subject. It turned out they never cleaned it. 'When we want to save something we just Xerox the table,' Hawking quipped."

Hawking in his office at the DAMTP.

would continue to do his actual work at the DAMTP in central Cambridge. He needed to live near his workplace, since he couldn't ride a bicycle or walk more than a short distance. In the 1960s, however, there was little public awareness of the needs of disabled people or of their right to access public facilities. The Cambridge authorities thought that the Hawkings' housing needs weren't their problem. The Hawkings were forced to find temporary quarters.

Their luck soon began to change, however. First they found a small house, less than a hundred yards from the DAMTP, that they could sublet for three months. A short time later an elderly neighbor who had made friends with the Hawkings found an empty house only a few doors farther down the street. Upset that such a nice young couple should be struggling to find permanent housing while a house stood empty nearby, the neighbor talked the house's owner into renting it to the Hawkings. The Hawkings later bought the house, and they lived there for many years. The house was tiny and cramped, but it became a real home, often crammed with friends sharing dinner and conversation.

Hawking's Condition Worsens

Hawking continued to make progress in following up his and Roger Penrose's first insights into singularities and black holes. In December 1965 the Hawkings again went to America, this time to deliver a talk about his and Penrose's work at a relativity

Hawking rides into the DAMTP in central Cambridge.

Over time, motor neuron disease has stripped Hawking of most of his physical powers. Nevertheless, Hawking manages to jet about the courts and streets of Cambridge.

meeting in Miami. By this time Hawking's voice had become quite slurred, and it was difficult for most people to understand him. Fortunately a good friend named George Ellis was also attending the meeting. He agreed to read Hawking's talk to the audience. The talk was very well received and brought Hawking's work on singularities to the attention of some of the world's greatest physicists. Only a few months after getting his Ph.D., Hawking found himself a member of a select group of researchers working on the frontiers of physics and cosmology.

Hawking's physical condition began to worsen in other ways. He had to trade in his walking stick for a pair of crutches. Getting up and down the stairs at home became difficult. One acquaintance was shocked to realize that Hawking now needed fifteen minutes to walk up one flight of stairs to his bedroom door. Soon Hawking had to abandon the crutches

and get around in a wheelchair, being carried when necessary.

Hawking refused to give up any more ground to his disease than he had to. Writer John Boslough described Hawking as "the toughest man I have ever met."[21] This determination and toughness could sometimes appear to be prickliness and arrogance. Jane notes that "some would call [his attitude] determination, some obstinacy. I've called it both at one time or another. I suppose that's what's kept him going."[22] Perhaps Jane's last point is the most important: Hawking made himself into the kind of person who could keep going despite the growing uselessness of his body. But it is also true that his attitude could be hard on friends who wanted only to help make his life easier, and it was especially hard on Jane, who increasingly had to help Hawking with his physical needs.

As Hawking's condition continued to worsen and the future appeared uncertain,

Hawking with his wife and three children at their Cambridge home. According to Jane, the birth of their first child "gave Stephen a great new impetus."

he and Jane felt that they could lose no more time if they wanted to start a family. Their first child, Robert, was born in 1967. According to Jane, the birth of Robert "obviously gave Stephen a great new impetus, being responsible for this tiny creature."[23] Robert was followed by a daughter, Lucy, in 1970, and another son, Timothy, in 1979.

Black Hole Breakthrough

In 1968 Hawking moved from the DAMTP to the Institute of Theoretical Astronomy (later the name was shortened to Institute of Astronomy). He obtained a car designed for disabled drivers so he could commute to the institute three times a week. By now he had his own office. As Hawking's work became better known, his presence began to attract visitors from all over the world. Simon Mitton, the head of the institute, described Hawking as "a human magnet in the world of physics."[24]

Once Hawking had shown that the universe must have begun with a singularity like that in a black hole, he turned his attention to black holes themselves. He soon realized that he had come up against a serious obstacle. There didn't seem to be much you could say about a black hole. A black hole has a mass and, therefore, gravitational attraction. The hole has a kind of shell around it called the event horizon, the boundary beyond which light or matter going near the hole would be sucked in forever. The event horizon has a radius that increases with the mass of the hole. The black hole might also be spinning. That was about it. No matter where a black hole had come from originally (a massive star, the heart of a galaxy, or something else entirely), it always ended up as a uniform object that had only mass, radius, and possibly spin. Physicists, using typically colorful language, summed up this situation by saying that a black hole has no hair. This meant that a black hole had no identifying characteristics that made it different from other black holes.

Hawking continued to struggle with these problems. Then he had an important realization:

> One evening, shortly after the birth of my daughter, Lucy, I started to think about black holes as I was getting into bed. My disability made this rather a slow process, so I had plenty of time. Suddenly I realized that the area of

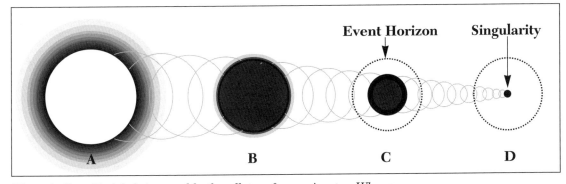

Theoretically, a black hole is caused by the collapse of a massive star. When a star runs out of fuel, it collapses on itself (A). Its gravitational force becomes so great that even light cannot escape, and it becomes invisible (B). The star continues to shrink, unlike the event horizon, the boundary beyond which light or matter is sucked in forever (C). The star continues to collapse until it is a single point with infinite density—a singularity (D).

the event horizon always increases with time. I was so excited with my discovery that I didn't get much sleep that night.[25]

Entropy

Why was it important that the area covered by a black hole's event horizon could only get bigger, never smaller? For one thing, it suggested for the first time that there was something about black holes that *did* change over time. Hawking then asked himself if this property of black holes was like anything else in the more familiar realms of physics. He found that there was a principle called entropy in the laws of thermodynamics that could be compared to the behavior of a black hole's event horizon.

Thermodynamics is basically the study of the flow of heat energy. The Second Law of Thermodynamics states that entropy always increases over time. Entropy is a measure of how disordered or disorga-

nized something is. The principle of entropy expresses our common experience that everything tends to wear out, run down, or get jumbled over time. Clothes get rumpled and dirty, papers on desks get mixed up, the bodies of people and animals wear out and eventually die. Even mountains that have stood for millions of years eventually erode or crumble away.

In physics entropy usually refers to the amount of heat energy in a system. For example, if you have just made a cup of coffee, the coffee is very hot—just under the boiling point of water. But after a few minutes the coffee cools. Eventually, the coffee reaches room temperature. The difference between the temperature of the coffee and that of the room has disappeared. Put another way, the energy in the room (expressed by heat, or the motion of molecules in the coffee and in the air) has become uniformly distributed. Instead of an ordered situation in which there is high energy in one place and low energy elsewhere, the energy has been jumbled so that it is everywhere. Entropy has increased.

Hawking's Way of Working

Science writer Dennis Overbye asked Hawking how his mind worked. This was his reply, as quoted in Overbye's book on twentieth-century astronomy, Lonely Hearts of the Cosmos:

"Sometimes I make a conjecture [conclusion] and then try to prove it. Many times, in trying to prove it, I find a counter-example, then I have to change my conjecture. Sometimes it is something that other people have made attempts on. I find that many papers are obscure and I simply don't understand them. So, I have to try to translate them into my own way of thinking. Many times I have an idea and start working on a paper and then I will realize halfway through that there's a lot more to it.

I work very much on intuition, thinking that, well, a certain idea ought to be right. Then I try to prove it. Sometimes I find I'm wrong. Sometimes I find that the original idea was wrong, but that leads to new ideas. I find it a great help to discuss my ideas with other people. Even if they don't contribute anything, just having to explain it to someone else helps me sort it out for myself."

Black Hole Thermodynamics

At first the existence of black holes seemed to violate the idea that the entropy of the universe as a whole was always increasing. Suppose you have a cup of hot tea and a glass of iced tea. Normally, if you place them so they touch, heat will pass from the cup of hot tea to the glass of iced tea. Physicists say that hotter always flows to colder. The difference in heat between the two containers will decrease, and thus the amount of entropy in the universe will increase a tiny bit.

But suppose there was a convenient black hole nearby, and you tossed both the cup and the glass into it? Since noth-ing can come out of a black hole, you have seemingly cheated the law of entropy. The amount of entropy in the universe would not, it seems, increase in this situation, because the inside of the black hole is sealed off from our ordinary universe. Any exception to a universal principle such as entropy is both disturbing and tantalizing to the scientific mind.

In order to puzzle out what was really going on with black holes and entropy, Hawking began to apply ideas from thermodynamics to black holes. This involved very complex mathematics, and by now Hawking could not write or type anything. Instead, he developed techniques for visualizing and memorizing the many intricate details in his head. A friend and colleague named Werner Israel described Hawking's achievement in dealing with black hole physics as being

> as though Mozart had composed and carried an entire symphony in his head—anyone who saw the lines of complex mathematics covering the blackboard like musical staves at a recent seminar would have appreciated the comparison.[26]

At first Hawking thought that the processes of thermodynamics could be used only as analogies to what might be going on in a black hole. (Analogies would be useful for understanding processes, but not for doing calculations or proving theories.) Thermodynamics deals mainly with gases of moving atoms, but in a black hole matter in the familiar form of molecules or even atoms does not exist.

Then a young researcher named Jacob Beckenstein, working at Princeton University, began applying thermodynamics directly to black holes. In particular, he said that the radius of the event horizon of a black hole directly measured the amount of entropy in the hole. The reason why black holes can't get smaller, he said, was because entropy could never decrease. The hot cup and the cold glass could not be hidden from the effects of entropy in a black hole: rather, their being swallowed up by the hole's gravity would result in an increase in the size of the event horizon, reflecting an increase in entropy.

At first Hawking thought Beckenstein's calculations were not justified. In reply to a paper by Beckenstein, Hawking and two colleagues published a paper with the title "The Four Laws of Black Hole Mechanics." Hawking pointedly used the

A black hole might look something like this as it pulls matter from nearby stars.

term *mechanics* rather than *thermodynamics* in his paper's title to show his disapproval of Beckenstein's use of thermodynamics. Hawking also pointed out that a black hole, since it could not emit any form of radiation, could not have a temperature. Since entropy is measured by temperature, Hawking said, a black hole couldn't have entropy in any meaningful way.

Hawking Radiation

In 1973, however, Hawking learned something that made him think again about Beckenstein's ideas. He made a trip to Moscow and visited a Soviet physicist named Yakov Boris Zel'dovich, who was studying the way the outside of black holes and light interact. Zel'dovich had reached the startling conclusion that a spinning black hole threw off particles. In other words, some black holes, at least, *could* emit radiation. Hawking thought that Zel'dovich and the other Russian researchers were on to something, but "I didn't like the way they derived their result, so I set out to do it properly."[27]

Thus far Hawking had been applying Einstein's theory of general relativity along with a bit of thermodynamics to black holes. Einstein's theory was one of the two powerful theories that had given twentieth-century physics the unprecedented ability to explain the behavior of matter and energy. The other breakthrough theory was that of quantum mechanics, first formulated in the 1920s, which explained how things worked in the world within the atom—a world of tiny particles, minuscule distances, and incredibly brief intervals of time.

For decades physicists had been living with the frustration of having two very useful theories—relativity and quantum mechanics—that dealt well with vastly different realms and did not seem to have anything to say to each other, because their languages were too different. Hawking decided that the only way he was going to make more progress with his study of black holes would be if he could somehow add the insights of quantum mechanics to what relativity had already told him.

When Hawking began to apply the equations of quantum mechanics to black holes, the results startled and distressed him. According to the equations black holes appeared to emit radiation, just as Zel'dovich had suggested. This meant that a black hole had a temperature and, therefore, could have entropy. Hawking confirmed the results of the Soviet research and extended it to apply to all black holes, not just spinning ones.

If a black hole's gravity trapped even light forever, how could a black hole emit radiation? The answer had to do with an aspect of quantum physics called the uncertainty principle. Simply put, this idea, which was developed by Werner Heisenberg in 1927, stated that there is a limit to how precisely the position of a particle of matter or wave of energy can be determined. You can calculate either the position of something or its velocity (direction and rate of motion) precisely, but not both. There is always a certain fuzziness when you reached extremely small distances and incredibly brief times.

This fuzziness means that even the so-called vacuum of space cannot be thought of as totally empty at the subatomic level. The vacuum can be filled with uncertain energy, which in turn can convert itself to

German physicist Werner Heisenberg developed the uncertainty principle, which states that there is a limit to how precisely the position of a particle of matter or wave of energy can be determined.

matter, in the form of pairs of particles. Each pair of particles consists of a particle and an antiparticle (a particle of antimatter, which scientists have created in tiny amounts in the laboratory and which powers the fictional starship *Enterprise* in *Star Trek*).

Normally such a pair of particles can exist only for an extremely brief interval of time before the particles collide and destroy each other, turning back into energy. But suppose a particle-antiparticle pair flashes into existence near the event horizon of a black hole, created from the gravitational energy there. In this case one particle might just have time to be captured by the hole. This means that its mate cannot collide with it but, instead, goes off into space in the form of radia-

tion. Since matter and energy are ultimately equivalent, this means that the black hole loses a tiny amount of mass.

For several months Hawking did not feel ready to share his problem with anyone. Then, in January 1974, in the middle of a dinner party to celebrate Hawking's thirty-second birthday, the phone rang. It was Roger Penrose calling from London. A few days earlier Hawking had told Dennis Sciama about his new conclusions about black holes. Sciama had told Penrose. The word had gotten around. Another colleague, running into Sciama in a corridor at Cambridge, excitedly told him "Have you heard? Stephen's changed everything!"[28]

Since his results were no longer a secret, Hawking agreed to announce them officially at a meeting in February. By the time the talk was over, you could hear a pin drop. The moderator of the meeting, physicist John Taylor, strongly disagreed with the idea of radiating black holes. He immediately began to write a paper to rebut Hawking's theory. Meanwhile, Hawking published a paper describing his ideas in *Nature*, a prestigious British scientific journal. Dennis Sciama described Hawking's paper as "one of the most beautiful in the history of physics."[29] Eventually the uproar died down, and the correctness of Hawking's new theories was accepted. The black hole radiation was named Hawking radiation in his honor.

Black Hole Explosions?

If black holes were slowly turning their mass into radiation, might a black hole eventually evaporate into space? Hawking's paper in *Nature*, provocatively entitled "Black Hole Explosions?" looked at this possibility.

Hawking believed that the ordinary kind of black hole, made from a massive star, pulled in matter from surrounding space much faster than it could lose it through emitting Hawking radiation. Starting in 1971, however, Hawking had begun thinking about a different kind of black hole. Anything that can create enough pressure on some matter can create a black hole—not just the collapsing mass of a huge star. In particular, Hawking began looking back at the Big Bang. His calculations suggested that if the universe that was created a tiny fraction of a second after the Big Bang wasn't completely uni-

form, differences in pressure would arise here and there. If such a difference were large enough, it could compress matter into mini black holes, objects perhaps as small as a proton, one of the particles that makes up an atom.

Miniholes behave differently from regular black holes in two ways. First, the smaller a black hole is, the more Hawking radiation it emits. (A minihole the size of a proton would put out about six thousand megawatts of energy, making it a great power plant. The only problem would be its unmanageable weight—although very tiny, the object would weigh about a billion tons.) Second, the smaller the hole, the less matter it can capture from surrounding space through its gravity.

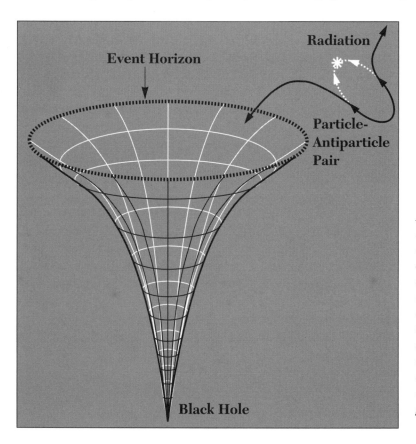

According to Hawking, black holes can emit radiation when conditions are just right. For example, a particle-antiparticle pair might be created near the event horizon of a black hole. Normally, these particles collide and annihilate one another. Near the event horizon, however, one particle might be captured by the black hole. Its mate then goes off into space emitting "Hawking" radiation.

Hawking near the time of his induction into the Royal Society—one of the world's most prestigious scientific organizations.

around the universe today. (Unfortunately, such explosions would be scattered over great distances of space and would be very hard to detect.)

A Fellow of the Royal Society

Only a few weeks after announcing his discovery of Hawking radiation, Stephen Hawking received an invitation to join the Royal Society, Britain's most prestigious scientific body, founded in 1660. Hawking, having just turned thirty-two years old, was one of the youngest scientists to receive this honor.

Traditionally, a newly appointed fellow of the Royal Society walks to the podium to sign the book that holds the names of Isaac Newton, Michael Faraday, and other scientific pioneers who have reshaped our understanding of the universe. The society's president brought the book to Stephen Hawking to sign. Writing in an excruciatingly slow, shaky hand, Hawking added his name to the membership roll. He considers this moment to be one of the high points of his career.

The result is that a minihole that is small enough will lose mass relatively rapidly and eventually explode. Hawking calculated that a number of miniholes should be exploding here and there

4 The Moment of Creation

During the 1970s Hawking continued to broaden his insights about black holes into a more general understanding of the origin of the universe and the nature of space and time. The discoveries of Hawking and other physicists and astronomers were quickly finding their way into popular culture. People who enjoyed *Star Trek* and the *Star Wars* films were also likely to be intrigued by stories about black holes or accounts of Stephen Hawking's search for answers to the ultimate mysteries of cosmic creation.

But for thousands of years religion had also claimed to explain the origin and meaning of the universe. Could scientific and religious explanations of the origin of the cosmos be brought into harmony with one another? A number of popular writers offered their own visions of quantum physics and mystical philosophy.

Even traditional religious organizations such as the Roman Catholic church joined in discussions of the new physics. In 1981 Pope John Paul II held a conference on cosmology at the Vatican in Rome. After the conference the visiting physicists and their spouses were invited to visit the pope at his summer home in the countryside.

The pope sat in a raised chair. Each visitor came up to the chair and knelt

while being introduced. When Stephen Hawking's turn came, however, he drove up to the pope in his electric wheelchair. The pope came down from his chair and knelt so that he could see Hawking face to

Pope John Paul II held a conference on cosmology at the Vatican in 1981. According to the pope, only the question of what happened before the beginning of the universe must remain forever beyond science.

Galileo is forced to renounce his views before the Catholic church in the seventeenth century. Although today—three centuries later—few restrictions are placed on scientific pursuit, the pope and others believe that some questions should remain divine mysteries.

face. Rather than just exchanging brief greetings, the two men talked together for what seemed like a long time. When the conversation ended, Pope John Paul II stood up with a smile.

Hawking must have keenly appreciated the irony in this meeting. He was born exactly three hundred years after Galileo, who in the first part of the seventeenth century had used a new invention, the telescope, to reveal the true nature of our solar system. According to Hawking:

> Galileo, perhaps more than any other single person, was responsible for the birth of modern science. His renowned conflict with the Catholic Church was central to his philosophy, for Galileo was one of the first to argue that man could hope to understand how the world works, and, moreover, that we could do this by observing the real world.[30]

Galileo's relationship with the church authorities had ended in a bitter silence. He had been forced to deny that the earth and the other planets orbited around the sun, despite the evidence he had gathered with his telescope. The fate of Galileo had

Why Not Think About the Unthinkable?

Stephen Hawking's mother, Isobel Hawking, isn't bothered by her son's sometimes strange-sounding theories and ideas. Rather, she seems to delight in them, as she says in A Reader's Companion:

"[Stephen] does believe very intensely in the almost infinite possibility of the human mind. You have to find out what you can't know before you know you can't, don't you? So I don't think that thought should be restricted at all. Why shouldn't you go on thinking about the unthinkable? Somebody has got to start sometime. How many things were unthinkable a century ago? Yet people have thought them—and often they also seem quite impractical. Not all the things Stephen says probably are to be taken as gospel truth. He's a searcher, he is looking for things. And if sometimes he may talk nonsense, well, don't we all? The point is, people must think, they must go on thinking, they must try to extend the boundaries of knowledge; yet they don't sometimes even know where to start."

seemed to set scientific observation and religious faith in direct opposition. But much had changed in three centuries. Now the pope and the church were inviting Hawking and other astronomers and physicists to pursue their research freely and vigorously. In his earlier address to the assembled scientists, the pope had said that only the question of what happened before the beginning of the universe must remain forever beyond science, being reserved for religious faith.

The pope probably didn't realize that the new theory Hawking had first unveiled at the Vatican conference attempted to answer just that forbidden question. Hawking's new view of space and time said that the universe might never have had a beginning. Hawking had reached this conclusion in the preceding years by combining in yet another way the con-

cepts of quantum mechanics and relativity that he had already used to explain black holes.

Quantum Space and Quantum Time

Following his discovery of black hole radiation in 1974, Hawking turned back to the question of what black holes might reveal about the Big Bang that most astronomers now believed had created our universe. As he continued to explore the quantum mechanics of black holes, he asked himself whether a black hole, or the universe before the Big Bang, really did contain a singularity as he and Penrose had thought in the 1960s. The surprising answer seemed to be no.

Quantum theory says that just as there is a fundamental uncertainty about the position of a particle, there is also a tiny but nonremovable uncertainty about the measurement of length and of time. This uncertainty is based on a number called Planck's constant, named after Max Planck, one of the founders of quantum mechanics. Planck's constant tells us that lengths shorter than 10^{-35} meters cannot be measured meaningfully, and no measurement of time can be shorter than 10^{-43} of a second. These are certainly very small numbers. (10^{-35}, for example, means a decimal point followed by thirty-four zeroes and a one.) But while unimaginably tiny, these quantities are *not* zero. Even in the heart of a black hole, it seemed, matter could not quite disappear completely and form a singularity.

There is no singularity inside a black hole after all, and a singularity could not have existed at the very moment of creation, the Big Bang. This means that the moment of creation might be understandable to science after all.

Hawking also found that the uncertainty principle had a strange effect on time just after the Big Bang. At the very beginning pressures were so high that space and time were crushed together into a single mysterious unit and had not yet separated into the familiar dimensions of our universe.

In the very early universe, when space was very compressed, the smearing effect of the uncertainty principle can change the basic distinction between space and time. . . . When this is the case, space and time lose their remaining distinction—we might say that time becomes fully spatialized—and it is then more accurate to talk, not of space-time, but of a four-dimensional space.[31]

We are used to thinking that space, but not time, can be shown on a map. But what happens when time becomes like space? For his next project, Hawking began to ask what a map combining space and time might look like. Perhaps such a map might tell the story of how the universe came to be. Hawking found a tool that he could use to answer this question—not at quiet Caius College, but in the very different world of Southern California.

German physicist Max Planck, one of the founders of quantum mechanics. Planck's theories were instrumental to Hawking as he pondered black holes and the beginning of the universe.

A Year in California

In the mid-1970s Hawking spent a year at Caltech, the California Institute of Technology, in Pasadena, California. Despite its relatively small size, Caltech is one of the world's great centers of research in science and technology.

In the 1970s Caltech had assembled an unlikely cast of characters for a scientific drama. Physicist Kip Thorne, his floral shirts and gray beard making him look a bit like a hippie guru left over from the 1960s, led an internationally renowned relativity research group. Thorne introduced Hawking to another physicist, Don Page, who became a lifelong friend and close collaborator. But probably the most important person Hawking met at Caltech was Richard Feynman, a Nobel Prize-winning quantum physicist.

Feynman was, in his own words, "a curious character." He delved deeply into physics by day and enthusiastically played bongo drums with college students in the evenings. Despite their very different cultural backgrounds, the British and American physicists found they got along well together. Both men shared a wry sense of humor and a fondness for practical jokes.

In his work with particle physics Feynman had developed a method for mapping the paths of particles in space-time. Quantum theory tells us that a particle such as an electron or photon (light particle) cannot be said to occupy a single, definite place in space-time. Rather, there are many possible paths the particle might take. The spreading out of these many possible paths makes these subatomic particles act like waves, setting up ripples and interference patterns. You can see interference patterns if you drop two rocks into a pond some distance apart, and watch what happens when the two approaching circles of ripples meet.

Not all paths that a particle can take are equally probable, however; only a few paths are at all likely at any given time. This fact keeps electrons whirling in their proper orbits around the nucleus of an atom, for example. Feynman's method, called sum of histories, involves calculating and mapping all of a particle's possible paths and assigning them probabilities. The result is a kind of map of the particle's possible presence in space-time.

Nobel Prize-winning Richard Feynman, a brilliant physicist and self-described "curious character." Hawking applied Feynman's sum of histories to the evolution of the entire universe.

Falling into a Black Hole

Science-fiction writers have written about spaceships plunging into one mini black hole and emerging from another far away. In Stephen Hawking: Quest for a Theory of Everything, *science writer Kitty Ferguson quotes Hawking as he points out a few problems with this form of space travel:*

"In real time, an astronaut who fell into a black hole would come to a sticky end. He would be torn apart by the difference between the gravitational force on his head and his feet. Even the particles that made up his body would not survive. Their histories, in real time, would come to an end at a singularity. However, the histories of the particles in imaginary time would continue. They would pass into the baby universe, and would re-emerge as the particles emitted by another black hole. Thus, in a sense, the astronaut would be transported to another region of the universe. However, the particles that emerged would not look much like the astronaut. Nor might it be much consolation to him, as he ran into the singularity in real time, to know that his particles would survive in imaginary time. The motto for anyone who falls into a black hole must be: Think Imaginary."

Matter is sucked into a black hole. Says Hawking, "An astronaut who fell into a black hole would come to a sticky end."

Boundless Space-Time

After learning about Feynman's techniques, Hawking had another one of the great leaps of intuition that seemed to mark each new stage in his career. What would happen, he thought, if the sum of histories technique was applied not to a single particle but to the evolution of the entire universe out of the Big Bang? Hawking could not make the calculations for each particle in the whole universe, of course—a computer the size of the earth could not do that. Instead, Hawking constructed a model based on a single particle moving in the kind of curved space-time that Einstein had described. When he determined the most probable path for such an ideal particle, the result

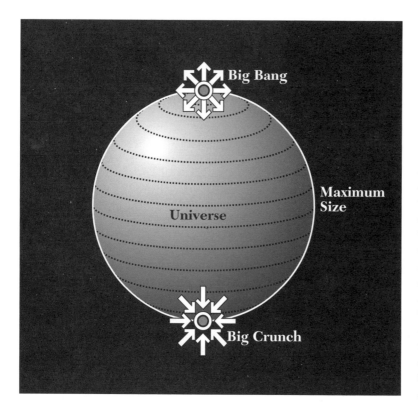

Big Bang

Universe

Maximum Size

Big Crunch

Hawking postulates that both space and time are unbounded, or curved. According to this model of the universe, if you move far enough in time from the Big Bang, you eventually come back to where you began. Hence, after the Big Bang, the universe expands to a very large size. After reaching a maximum size, it begins to collapse until it is compressed to a very high density—the Big Crunch.

was a space-time that was curved and boundless. What does this mean?

The best way to imagine boundless space-time is to picture the history of the universe spread out on a globe of the world. On the globe the expansion of the universe is represented by the circles of latitude that go around the earth, which grow larger as you move south toward the equator. Time is represented by a line of longitude, moving southward from the North Pole.

The North Pole represents the point of creation—the Big Bang. As you move southward along the time line, the circles around the earth get bigger. This corresponds to the steadily expanding universe. The universe reaches its largest extent at the equator. Then, as time continues toward the South Pole, the universe begins

to shrink or contract. At the South Pole the universe is again compressed to a very high density. (This state, the opposite of the Big Bang, has been dubbed the Big Crunch. A Big Crunch is just a Big Bang approached from the other side.)

The important thing about this model of the universe is that it is unbounded in both space and time. Space is curved so that going straight in any direction will eventually get you back to your starting point. Time is also curved: if you move far enough in time from the Big Bang, you eventually come back to where you began.

Hawking first announced his newly worked out model of the universe at the Vatican conference in 1981. He then published a paper on it, written with James Hartle, in 1983. In talking about this model, Hawking stresses that it has not yet been proven to be true. At the same time, Hawking says it does correctly predict the phenomena that astronomers had been observing as they studied the early universe: an explosion at the beginning followed by rapid expansion.

Hawking also says that his theory especially appeals to him because of what it says about science itself: "It really underlies science because it is really the statement that the laws of science hold everywhere."[32]

The idea of boundless space-time would seem to be a direct challenge to the boundary between science and religion set by the pope. The pope had said that what went on before the Big Bang—the beginning of time—was a divine mystery. But Hawking's theory said that time had no beginning: the Big Bang was like a point on an endless circle:

> So long as the universe had a beginning, we could suppose that it had a creator. But if the universe is really completely self-contained, what place, then, for a creator?[33]

Hawking's conclusion might well trouble some religious people. In particular, it upset Jane Hawking, whose strong religious faith had helped her meet the challenge of caring for a disabled husband and a growing family. Other religious

---

Can Time Run Backwards?

Hawking at first thought that a boundless, curved space-time might mean that at some time in the future of the universe time might begin to run backwards. In A Reader's Companion *he recounts the development of his thoughts about time:*

"What would happen if and when the universe stopped expanding and began to contract? Would the thermodynamic arrow [of time] reverse and disorder begin to decrease with time? Would we see broken cups gather themselves together off the floor and jump back onto the table? Would we be able to remember tomorrow's prices and make a fortune off the stock market? I felt that the universe had to return to a smooth and ordered state when it recollapsed. If this were so, people in the contracting phase would live their lives backwards. They would die before they were born and get younger as the universe got small again. Eventually, they would disappear back into the womb. . . .

I had made a mistake. It turned out I was using too simple a model of the universe. Time will not reverse direction when the universe begins to contract. People will continue to get older, so it is no good waiting until the universe recollapses to return to our youth."

As astronomers continue to inspect regions of space, they find that matter seems to be distributed quite evenly.

thinkers might, however, still say that God created the universe from a place outside Hawking's circle of time. Hawking has wisely stayed away from such religious questions.

The Inflatable Universe

The 1980s found Hawking looking at yet another cosmological question: how did the Big Bang give us the kind of universe we see today? In particular, as astronomers have looked at larger and larger volumes of space, they have found that matter in the form of stars and galaxies seems to be distributed quite evenly or uniformly throughout space. Further, the microwave background radiation that helped prove the Big Bang theory turned out to have

the same temperature no matter where it was measured. Why is this so?

An intriguing answer was proposed by a young researcher named Alan Guth, who worked at Cornell University in New York. Guth suggested that the universe immediately after the Big Bang had a tremendous amount of energy held in a kind of suspended state by the laws of quantum mechanics. This balance was highly unstable, however, and something gave way. The universe then expanded at an incredible rate of speed, going in a tiny fraction of a second from the size of a proton, far smaller than an atom, to a kind of bubble of energy about the size of a grapefruit. The energy turned into heat, and the grapefruit-sized cosmic fireball gave us the Big Bang, the creation of matter, and the universe.

According to this inflation theory, the universe today is so uniform because it started out too small to have any bumps or irregularities. Further, the inflation might have given the hot matter enough time to mix evenly, meanwhile flattening out space in somewhat the way that a wrinkled balloon becomes smooth as you blow air into it. This and similar ideas have been called cosmic bubble theories.

Hawking helped Guth work out some of the details of the new theory, although the major work was done by a Soviet physicist named Andrei Linde.

Inflation and Hawking Radiation

Another young researcher, J. Richard Gott of Princeton University in New Jersey, built on Hawking's earlier work with black holes. Gott has attempted to use something very similar to the Hawking radiation at the event horizon of a black hole to explain another aspect of the Big Bang.

Because the inflating universe was expanding too rapidly for light to get from one side of it to the other, light was in effect trapped on one side of a boundary much like the event horizon around a black hole. Gott suggested that event horizons constantly formed during the inflation process. The event horizons, like those around black holes, caused pairs of particles to be split apart, producing heat energy similar to Hawking radiation. Gott's most intriguing suggestion is that the leftover part of this radiation, following the creation of the matter of the universe, forms the background microwave radiation that we detect today.

As Hawking continued to work with cosmic bubbles and inflation, he looked at a problem with early versions of the inflation theory:

> The thing is that if you form bubbles, then you are liable to come up with more than one bubble. And these bubbles are likely to collide. And this will give rise to a [nonuniform] universe. And that is not consistent with what we observe today.[34]

Hawking first investigated the suggestion of Andrei Linde, the Soviet researcher,

Why Are Things the Way They Are?

If there is more than one universe, what makes our particular universe the way it is? In Stephen Hawking's Universe *by John Boslough, Hawking takes an anthropic, or human-centered, approach to this question:*

"This principle can be paraphrased as, 'Things are as they are because we are.'

According to one version of the principle, there is a large number of different and separate universes. Each has different values for its physical parameters and for its initial conditions. Most will not have the right conditions for the development of intelligent life.

However, in a small number there will be conditions and parameters as in our universe. In those, it will be possible for intelligent life to develop and ask the question 'Why is the universe as we observe it?' The only answer will be that if it were otherwise, there would be nobody to ask the question.

Surprisingly, this principle provides some explanation of many of the remarkable numerical relations that are observed between the values of different physical parameters."

that only a single bubble might have formed. If true, that would remove the problem of collisions and the resulting irregularities. But Hawking was not satisfied with Linde's theory. Working with a colleague named Ian Moss, Hawking developed a different explanation. The earlier inflation theorists had simplified their work by assuming a flat space-time. Hawking and Moss, however, used the curved space-time that came from relativity theory. This, they announced, resulted in a smooth rather than a lumpy universe.

In July 1982 Hawking and other cosmologists met at a conference at Cambridge to discuss these startling new ideas about the very early universe. The conference attempted to deal with other problems with the inflation idea that still remain today. These problems deal mainly with explaining exactly how inflation from a bubble could create the universe as we know it today: basically uniform, yet filled with the varied details of galaxies and star clusters.

Where Physics Meets Science Fiction

Perhaps the strangest idea coming out of the bubble inflation theory, however, is that there may be many universes rather than just one. Gott and Linde have suggested that under the right conditions there might have been many bubbles formed in the super fast expansion of the Hawking radiation from the event horizons at the beginning of creation. In this view, even if two bubbles formed close to each other, they will be forced apart by the speed of the expansion and would not collide. Each bubble would then have its own Big Bang and form a separate universe with its own physical laws.

A different multiple universe theory says that another universe could be created as a kind of bud pinched off from our space-time. From the outside, this baby universe would look like a tiny black

Do wormholes exist? A new generation of astronomers think they might. Below is an artist's conception of two kinds of wormholes. On the left, a wormhole leads from one universe to another. The wormhole on the right connects one part of a universe with another part that is millions of light-years away.

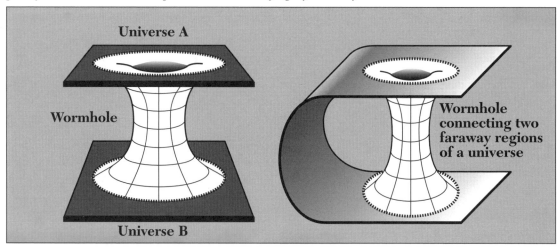

Universe A

Wormhole

Universe B

Wormhole connecting two faraway regions of a universe

hole—a wormhole. The inside, however, could stretch into a space-time as big as our own. This means that *our* universe might be inside a black hole in some other universe! Science fiction writers eagerly seized on these ideas and wrote stories in which people traveled to alternate universes or jumped from one part of our universe to another by way of a convenient pair of wormholes, ignoring the limitation of the speed of light.

As the 1980s moved on, it became clear that a kind of Big Bang had occurred in the study of cosmology. A new generation of researchers had taken Hawking's ideas about singularities, Hawk-ing radiation, and boundless space-time in a variety of different directions. These ideas, with their science fictional flavor, intrigued the general public in an age of space exploration and high technology.

Unfortunately, many of the ideas that Hawking and his colleagues were working on were hard to understand. Hawking felt that popular explanations sometimes distorted them. He therefore decided to write a book for nonscientists in which he would describe what was known or might someday be known about the universe. Before he could finish his book, however, he would have a brush with death and lose his voice for good, only to gain another one.

5 A Brief History of Time

In July 1985 Stephen Hawking decided to spend some time visiting with fellow physicists at CERN, the European Council for Nuclear Research in Geneva, Switzerland. This major research center has some of the world's finest physicists and equipment. In particular, CERN's powerful particle accelerator could smash particles together at very high energies. By studying the interactions of the particles, physicists might be able to confirm some of their new theories.

By this time Hawking needed both a full-time nurse and a live-in research assistant to enable him to carry on his work, or indeed, to survive at all. Hawking's physical condition had been slowly getting worse. For some time, he had been unable to feed himself, dress, or make more than facial and limited finger movements. His voice could no longer be understood by anyone who had not lived and worked with him for a long time. Hawking's nurse and assistant had to be his hands and his interpreter to the outside world.

One night while Hawking was in Geneva, his nurse checked on him in his bedroom, as she did every half hour while he

In 1985 Hawking visited with some of the world's finest physicists at CERN, the European Council for Nuclear Research in Geneva, Switzerland.

Hawking and the New Age

Black holes have fascinated many New Age spiritual and psychological writers. In Lonely Hearts of the Cosmos *Dennis Overbye suggested to Hawking a connection between black holes and the story of the Hindu goddess Kali's swallowing up and then giving birth to the universe. Hawking responded as follows:*

"It's fashionable rubbish. People go overboard on Eastern mysticism simply because it's something different that they haven't met before. But, as a natural description of reality, it fails abysmally. . . . If you look through Eastern mysticism you can find things that look suggestive of modern physics or cosmology. I don't think they have any significance.

Calling these things black holes was a master-stroke by Wheeler because it does make a [psychological] connection, or conjure up a lot of human neuroses [mental disorders]. If the Russian term "frozen star" had been generally adopted, then this part of Eastern mythology would not at all seem significant. They're named black holes because they relate to human fears of being destroyed or gobbled up."

slept. She immediately saw that he seemed to be choking. His face had turned violet. She called an ambulance, which rushed Hawking to the hospital. He was immediately put on a ventilator, a machine to help him breathe.

Hawking was very lucky to have a modern hospital nearby. According to some later reports the doctor in charge of treating Hawking had just seen a TV documentary about the disabled physicist. The TV show had explained that Hawking had suffered from ALS. Having learned this, the doctor knew what drugs he could safely use to treat Hawking.

As Hawking lay in the intensive care ward, doctors tried to find the cause of his breathing problems. One possibility was particularly worrisome: pneumonia. This infection causes the lungs and airways to fill with fluid. It is usually easy to treat, but it can be fatal for a person who has already been weakened by a condition such as ALS. Meanwhile, the medical staff tried to contact Jane Hawking, who was touring in Germany with friends. They finally tracked her down.

When Jane arrived at the hospital, the doctors told her that she would have to make a difficult decision. Because of the obstruction in his windpipe. Stephen could not breathe through his nose or mouth. The doctors could perform an operation called a tracheostomy to open a hole in the windpipe below the obstruction, allowing Hawking to breathe again. Indeed, the doctors told Jane that without this operation, Stephen would probably die. The operation, however, would permanently remove Hawking's ability to speak or make any kind of vocal sound. Jane recalls:

> The future looked very, very bleak. We didn't know how we were going to be able to survive—or if he was going to survive. It was my decision for him to have a tracheostomy. But I have sometimes thought, what have I done? What sort of life have I let him in for?[35]

Jane was concerned about more than her husband's physical survival. How would he be able to work if he could no longer speak, even through an interpreter? Would his still functioning mind be trapped inside a helpless body that was unable to do more than blink or twitch a finger? And if Hawking could not work, how could they afford the tremendous expense of year after year of full-time care?

Ironically, the loss of Hawking's voice came just when he was working on a project that would enable him to communicate with millions of people in a way that he had never attempted before. For the past several years Hawking had been working on a book that would explain step by step, in terms that nonscientists could understand, the story of how the universe came to be, and of the principles that made it that way.

Popular Science

By the early 1980s Hawking realized that he needed greater financial security. He had to have money both to pay for his full-time nursing care and to put his daughter Lucy through college. Given his medical

Fred Hoyle's success with popular science books encouraged Hawking to begin writing an account of his own work.

condition, getting any kind of life or health insurance was out of the question. He had to find another way to provide for the future if he died or could no longer work. His salary at Cambridge was far less than what other famous universities and institutes around the world, eager to have such a famous scientist on their faculty, had offered him. Still, he liked Cambridge and didn't want to leave it.

Around the end of 1982 Hawking decided that writing a popular science book might go a long way toward solving his money problems. Popular interest in science was strong: other scientists and science writers, such as Fred Hoyle and Arthur Eddington, had already written successful books on the new cosmology. Hawking also felt that writing a popular book would give him a chance to explain things in his own words and correct what he thought were the distortions that had crept into popular accounts of his work.

The Making of a Book

Hawking first approached Cambridge University Press with his book idea. Cambridge had already published several of his technical science books. Simon Mitton, an experienced science writer and editor who worked for the press, agreed that a popular book by Stephen Hawking would probably be a big seller.

Mitton's experience made him keenly aware of what would and would not work in writing for a popular audience. When Hawking showed him a sample section of his proposed book, Mitton told him that what he had written was much too technical and complicated for the general public. He explained to Hawking that a popular science book was "like baked beans. The blander the flavour, the broader the market. There simply isn't a commercial niche for specialist books like this." [36]

Hawking tried to simplify his writing. When he showed the manuscript to Mitton again, the editor told him that it was still far too technical. "Look at it this way, Steve—every equation will halve your sales." When Hawking asked Mitton what he meant, he explained:

Well, when people look at a book in a shop, they just flick through it to decide if they want to read it. You've got equations on practically every page. When they look at this, they'll say, "This book's got sums in it," and put it back on the shelf. [37]

Hawking and Mitton negotiated a tentative contract for the book. Hawking, keeping his money needs in mind, drove a hard bargain. Meanwhile Peter Guzzardi, an editor at Bantam Books in New York, saw a newspaper article about Stephen Hawking. A colleague of Guzzardi's, literary agent Al Zuckerman, had already learned that Hawking was planning to write a science book. Guzzardi asked Zuckerman to try to talk Hawking into letting Bantam publish the book.

Zuckerman contacted Hawking just as he was about to sign the final contract with Cambridge University Press. The agent persuaded Hawking that Bantam, a large American publisher specializing in popular books, was much better equipped than Cambridge to give Hawking's book the public exposure it would need for big sales. To get Hawking the best deal possible, however, Zuckerman offered Hawking's book at auction to the highest bidder. Bantam won with a high bid of $250,000 guaranteed in advance, plus a high royalty fee to be paid on each copy sold. This deal amounted to more than ten times what Cambridge had offered.

Like Mitton, Guzzardi was concerned that Hawking's book would be too technical to attract a mass audience:

I read the manuscript and thought it was very interesting . . . but that it would not be readily comprehensible to the lay reader. . . . I thought at that time that we should bring in a professional writer to help put the ideas across in language which would be more easily understood. Hawking refused; he wanted the book to be all his. And he is a very strong-minded man. [38]

Steps to Understanding

Because his condition made speech difficult and writing impossible, Hawking was used to dictating his thoughts to his assistants in as few words as possible. This meant that the connections between ideas—how one step in a theory led to the next one—weren't always explained clearly. Hawking and Guzzardi went through a tedious process in which each chapter was painstakingly written by Hawking with the help of his assistants. Guzzardi then sent it back with detailed criticism and questions, and the process repeated itself. Zuckerman has said:

> I would guess that, for every page of text Peter [Guzzardi] wrote two to three pages of editorial letters, all in an attempt to get Hawking to elaborate on ideas that his mind jumps over, but other people wouldn't understand.[39]

Hawking admits that the editing was necessary and that the final product "is a much better book as a result."[40]

Although popular writing was a new experience for Hawking, he brought some important strengths to the creation of the book. The very limitations that sometimes made his discussion hard to follow also resulted in precise language that zeroed in on the most vital questions. For example, Hawking decided to call his book *A Brief History of Time.* This title might seem peculiar at first glance. History, of course, is the study of how events such as wars or migrations take place *in* time. But what did Hawking mean by a history *of* time?

One thing he meant is that understanding time might be the key to understanding the universe. Asking about the history of time—did it have a beginning and will it have an end?—is equivalent to asking about the origin and fate of the universe itself. Hawking sums up the central questions like this:

> Which came first, the chicken or the egg? Did the universe have a beginning, and if so, what happened before then? Where did the universe come from, and where is it going?[41]

Hawking's investigation of the Big Bang and quantum mechanics had suggested that the universe may not have had a beginning. Instead, the history of time may be like a vast circle that closes in on itself after billions of years.

A Historical Perspective

A Brief History of Time is also a history of the *idea* of time. In it, Hawking describes how scientists have, step by step, uncovered the secrets of the universe and of the atoms from which all matter is made. Beginning with ancient Greek philosophers and continuing through Galileo's observations and Newton's laws of gravity to the twentieth-century discoveries of Einstein and the quantum physicists, he builds up a picture of the forces and relationships that are at work in planets, stars, and atoms. Hawking fits his own discoveries about black holes and the Big Bang into this unfolding picture. Hawking's book closes with chapters that discuss the nature of time, the possible development of a single theory that could explain all the forces in physics, and the fate of the universe.

The result is challenging reading, but Hawking has taken the advice about not having sums in his book: the only equation that appears is Einstein's classic $E=mc^2$. Instead of equations, Hawking relies on analogies and diagrams to show relationships and movement in space and time. His years of having to work in a highly visual way have provided another strength in helping him communicate with a popular audience.

A New Voice

Hawking's illness and the loss of his voice came just as the editing of his book was almost complete. Stephen and Jane didn't yet know how successful the book would be. The cost of intensive medical and nursing care might soon exhaust their savings. (The national health care program run by the British government provided only a fraction of the care necessary.) Jane immediately began writing letters to charitable foundations around the world, seeking possible benefactors. An American foundation agreed to pay $50,000 a year toward Hawking's support. Other foundations followed with smaller donations.

Perhaps the most important kind of support came from a different direction. The 1980s brought powerful computers to people's desktops and homes. A California computer expert named Walt Woltosz had written a program called Equalizer. This program, which can run on commonly available desktop computers, lets the operator select words from the screen. As menus of likely choices scroll by, a squeeze of the hand selects the desired word from a three thousand-word vocabulary. The

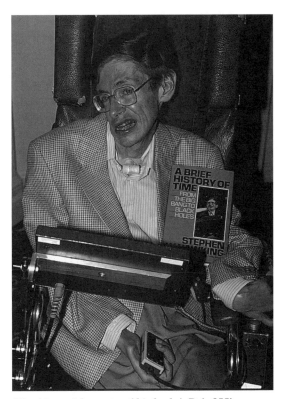

Hawking with a copy of his book A Brief History of Time, *in which he explores the nature of time and the origin of the universe. Few predicted how successful the book would be.*

words are built up into sentences, which are then articulated by a voice synthesizer. The system also includes a number of preprogrammed requests that could be triggered quickly without the tedium of selecting each word. Words that aren't in the built-in vocabulary can also be spelled out a letter at a time. Woltosz, knowing about Hawking's needs, sent him a copy of the program.

With Equalizer, Hawking found that he could speak ten words a minute; he later increased his speed to fifteen. "It was a bit slow, but then I think slowly, so it suited me quite well," he said.[42] It was also far better than the only other communications device that had been available to him after he lost his voice, a plastic board with which he used eye movements to spell out words a letter at a time. Hawking could now speak to anyone in an understandable voice. There was only one minor problem with the vocal quality: Hawking began to greet his visitors by saying, "Hello, please excuse my American accent."[43]

The computer software could also be used for writing, so Hawking no longer had to dictate his thoughts to an assistant. Soon a smaller computer that could run the program was fitted into Hawking's electric wheelchair. As had been the case with some of his earlier medical setbacks,

Hawking had ended up better off in some ways than he had before. He could communicate better than ever.

A Best-Seller

A Brief History of Time: From the Big Bang to Black Holes went to the bookstores in the spring of 1988. By then Guzzardi had left Bantam, and a different editor had been placed in charge of the book's promotion and sales. The new editor decided that the book was still too difficult for a mass audience and probably wouldn't sell well. As a

Hawking lectures to a roomful of students, a task made possible by a computer program called Equalizer. To use Equalizer, Hawking uses his computer to select words which are then articulated by a voice synthesizer.

Reply to a Critic

When a newspaper columnist claimed that he couldn't get beyond page 29 of Hawking's A Brief History of Time, *and other writers speculated about how many copies of the book were actually being read after purchase, Isobel Hawking wrote a letter to the editor of* Independent *magazine. The quote is excerpted from* Stephen Hawking: A Life in Science:

"Sir: I have to declare an interest, as I am the mother of Professor Stephen Hawking, but I have given some thought to the reasons for the success of *A Brief History of Time* . . . a success which surprised Stephen himself. I believe the reasons to be complex, but shall attempt to simplify them—as I see them.

The book is well-written, which makes it pleasurable to read. The ideas are difficult, not the language. It is totally non-pompous; at no time does he talk down to his readers. He believes that his ideas are accessible to any interested person. . . .

Certainly his fight against illness has contributed to the book's popularity, but Stephen had come a long way before the book was even thought of. He did not collect his academic and other distinctions because of motor neuron disease.

I do not claim to understand the book myself, though I did read it to the end before coming to this conclusion. I think my age and type of mental training have something to do with my non-comprehension. Without wishing to doubt the brilliance of Mr. Levin's intellect, I should hesitate to assume from his non-comprehension that most people share it."

Stephen with his mother Isobel, who comments on the success of A Brief History of Time.

An Unlikely Blockbuster

Book reviewer Simon Jenkins of the London Sunday Times *is quoted in White and Gribbin's biography,* Stephen Hawking: A Life in Science:

"I am all but mystified. Throughout this summer, a book by a 46-year-old Cambridge math professor on the problem of equating relativity theory with quantum mechanics has been on the British non-fiction best-seller list. For the past month it has been top. Michael Jackson and Pablo Picasso have been toppled. Stephen Hawking's *A Brief History of Time* has notched up five reprints and 50,000 copies in hardback. This is blockbuster territory."

result, the book received little advertising, and far fewer copies were printed than had been originally planned.

Just a few days after publication an editor noticed that two pictures had been accidentally put in the wrong place when the book had been assembled. The sales staff began calling big bookstores and asking them to send their copies back for replacement. To their surprise, the publishers were told that there *were* no copies to send back. They had all been sold. A corrected, reprinted edition was rushed to the stores.

By the summer of 1988 *A Brief History of Time* had been on the American best-seller lists for four months and had sold half a million copies. When the book was published in Britain in June 1988, sales were very brisk there as well. Hawking was deluged with requests for interviews. Hawking told one interviewer:

I am pleased a book on science competes with the memoirs of pop stars. Maybe there is still hope for the human race. I am very pleased for it to

Hawking with Hollywood film producer Errol Morris, who brought A Brief History of Time *to the big screen.*

reach the general public, not just academics. It is important that we all have some idea of what science is about because it plays such a big role in modern society.[44]

Hawking now found himself becoming a sort of pop star. In the next few years a Hollywood film producer created a movie version of the book that turned out to be quite popular. In an age where "sound bites" and MTV are supposed to be all that can fit the attention span of the public, a surprising number of people have gone to theaters or, later, watched the home video to hear the slow, mechanical voice of Stephen Hawking explaining his work, together with the comments of many of his friends and colleagues.

The popularity of *A Brief History of Time* encouraged Bantam Books in 1993 to publish a collection of Hawking's earlier writings—essays, talks, and interviews—with the title *Black Holes and Baby Universes*. While *A Brief History of Time* focuses on scientific matters, the new book includes autobiography and even a discussion of Hawking's favorite music in addition to the exploration of scientific questions.

Hawking's newfound popularity has both provided him with new opportunities and saddled him with new problems.

6 Fame and Mixed Blessings

As the 1980s drew to a close, Stephen Hawking's fame grew by leaps and bounds. In Chicago a Stephen Hawking fan club began selling T-shirts with his picture on them. Magazine articles and television documentaries about him came out seemingly every month, bearing titles like "Master of the Universe" and "Courageous Physicist Knows the Mind of God." In 1993 Hawking even found his way into science fiction: in a brief appearance on the TV show "Star Trek: the Next Generation," he matched wits with Einstein, Newton, and the android Data in a poker game. (Hawking won the hand.) Thanks to the efforts of the media, many people who knew nothing else about physics could now name at least two physicists: Albert Einstein and Stephen Hawking.

Hawking before a portrait of his famous predecessor Isaac Newton. In 1979 Hawking was appointed Lucasian Professor of Mathematics at Cambridge. Newton held the post several centuries earlier.

A Scientific Superstar

Hawking had also continued to collect numerous awards over the years. In 1978 he was given the Albert Einstein Award, considered by many to be as important in physics as the Nobel Prize. In 1979 Hawking was appointed the Lucasian Professor of Mathematics at Cambridge. His most famous predecessor in that position was Isaac Newton, who had held the post about three hundred years earlier.

Queen Elizabeth II of Great Britain made Hawking a Companion of Honor, one of the highest honors the nation can

A Hawking family portrait. As Hawking approached his fiftieth birthday, he enjoyed worldwide admiration and a loving family—a remarkable feat for a man who, in 1963, was given only a few years to live.

give, in 1989. On the day of the award ceremony an orchestra played a special concert in Hawking's honor. Prince Philip presented the award to Hawking. Crowds lined the streets and applauded as Hawking's wheelchair rolled along in the company of some of Britain's most famous people. One reporter described the scene:

> There were tears rolling down the cheeks of men and women as a tribute to [Hawking's] courage, as well as [to] the exceptional brain which has continued to advance knowledge of time and space in spite of the ravages of a crippling disease.[45]

As Hawking approached his fiftieth birthday, he seemed to have gained so much: awards, honors, fame, a best-selling book, and a loving family. But the extent of Hawking's fame gives rise to important questions. What role did Hawking's disability play in his success? Would Hawking have been so richly honored if he had not suffered from such a crippling disease? Can Hawking's achievements as a scientist and his virtues and faults as a human be-

ing be separated from the heroic legend that has grown up around him? Have fame and fortune been good or bad for Stephen Hawking, or some of both?

A Scientist First

Hawking is certainly aware of the attention that has been paid to his physical condition, and he is not entirely happy about it. As Michael White and John Gribbin point out in their biography of him:

> Stephen Hawking does not like to dwell too much on his disabilities, and even less on his personal life. He would rather people thought of him as a scientist first, popular science writer second, and, in all the ways that matter, a normal human being with the same desires, drives, dreams and ambitions as the next person.[46]

It may be difficult to look at Hawking as he would like people to see him, however. Another of Hawking's biographers,

Kitty Ferguson, notes that after the tremendous success of *A Brief History of Time,*

> There was an occasional hint of sour grapes, a half-suppressed mutter of "His work's no different from [that of] a lot of other physicists; it's just that his condition makes him interesting." But there has been surprisingly little of that. Hawking can more than hold his own in any company, and everyone knows it. Moreover, his colleagues enjoy him.[47]

Ferguson tries to put Hawking's disability into perspective with his life and work.

> However, it isn't unreasonable to suggest that Hawking's scientific accomplishments alone would never have made him the celebrity he is or sold millions of books. . . . The truth is, although Hawking would almost certainly prefer it otherwise, most of the world probably appreciates him more for his spirit than for his scientific achievements.[48]

But it may be impossible to separate Hawking's disability from those scientific achievements, or at least from the shape they took. Hawking, looking back at it all, told an interviewer:

> I think I'm happier now than I was before I started. Before the illness set in I was very bored with life. I drank a fair amount, I guess, didn't do any work. It was really a rather pointless existence. When one's expectations are reduced to zero, one really appreciates everything that one does have.[49]

Hawking seems to have used his disability as a kind of discipline, an obstacle that gave him something to push against in shaping his life and work. Certainly, it prompted him to form a very strong and determined personality. Hawking also says "If you are disabled physically, you cannot afford to be disabled psychologically."[50] And when another interviewer asked Hawking whether he ever got depressed when thinking about his disability, he replied, "Not normally. I have managed to

Although the ravages of disease have left Hawking with little physical power, his mind remains active and brilliant.

Hawking is an advocate for the rights of the disabled. He says of his disability: "If you are disabled physically, you cannot afford to be disabled psychologically."

do what I wanted to do despite it, and that gives me a feeling of achievement."[51]

Hawking's disability also affected the way that he worked. Since communication with people around him was tedious and difficult, Hawking learned to create precise and elaborate pictures in his mind that summarized rows of complicated equations. It is sometimes hard to separate disability from ability.

An Advocate for the Disabled

Hawking thus appears to be at peace with himself about his condition. He has also, over the years, become a more active advocate for the rights of disabled people. Perhaps he has done so in part because he remembers how he had once suffered university authorities' indifference to his needs. Hawking told a conference on occupational help for the disabled:

> It is very important that disabled children should be helped to blend with others of the same age. It determines their self-image. How can one feel a member of the human race if one is set apart from an early age? It is a form of apartheid [segregation]. Aids like wheelchairs and computers can play an important role in overcoming physical deficiencies; the right attitude is even more important. It is no use complaining about the public's attitude about the disabled. It is up to disabled people to change people's awareness in the same way that blacks and women have changed public perceptions.[52]

Hawking has joined efforts to improve disabled people's access to public facilities. His unique position makes him a natural spokesperson for the disabled—one that is hard to ignore.

The Human Side

Stephen Hawking's personality includes much more than grim determination, however. A robust sense of humor is also part of the Hawking legend. The door to an office Hawking once shared with a colleague bore a sign that read "Black Holes Are Out of Sight." A sign on the door to his new office reads "QUIET PLEASE, THE BOSS IS ASLEEP."

Hawking's visitors often remark how expressive his body language is, even though it is limited to facial movements. He has also made his wheelchair into an extension of his body. He loves to whirl the chair around on a dance floor. When someone says something Hawking doesn't like, the wheelchair often goes into action, expertly nipping at the toes of the offender.

Whether someone calls Hawking's attitude determined or stubborn often depends on whether the person is on the receiving end of it. In one case Hawking's stubbornness resulted in genuine harm. It began in 1981, when Hawking was leading a seminar in which, according to Hawking, he mentioned his recent work with Andrei Linde on a new variation in the theory of cosmic inflation. A young professor named Paul Steinhardt was in the audience. In February 1982 Steinhardt and a student, Andreas Albrecht, sent Hawking a paper that contained ideas very similar to those of Linde that Hawking had mentioned at the seminar the year before. Hawking responded by claiming that Steinhardt had heard these ideas at his seminar. His implication was that Steinhardt had plagiarized, or stolen, Linde's ideas, claiming them as his own. This is a very serious charge to make against any scientist. Such an accusation from Hawking could seriously damage Steinhardt's career.

Steinhardt denied that he had heard about Linde's ideas at Hawking's seminar. He also accused Hawking of going behind his back with his charges, rather than raising them openly where they could be resolved in public. Hawking apologized to Steinhardt, and the matter seemed settled. In 1988, however, the same charges turned up again in *A Brief History of Time*. Steinhardt at the time was exploring the possibility of getting a grant from the National Science Foundation. A foundation official saw the passage in Hawking's book, ending any possibility of Steinhardt's receiving the grant.

Steinhardt now had to defend his reputation in public. Looking through his office, he found a videotape of Hawking's 1981 seminar. The tape showed that Hawking had not discussed Linde's ideas in the seminar after all, so Steinhardt couldn't have learned them there. Hawking agreed to remove the incorrect account from future editions of *A Brief History of Time*, but at first he neither admitted that he had been wrong nor offered to apologize. Finally, after colleagues around the world worked to convince him that he had been wrong, Hawking relented and issued a full correction and apology.

This incident shows the negative side of Hawking's famous stubbornness. As Hawking's daughter Lucy notes:

I think a lot of people don't realize just how stubborn [he] is. Once he gets an idea in his head, he will follow it through no matter what the consequences are. He doesn't let a thing drop. He will do what he wants to do at any cost to anybody else.[53]

That same relentless following through of an idea, of course, led Hawking to one great scientific breakthrough after another. And bitter disputes are not unusual in the history of science—Isaac Newton, for example, was often embroiled with one rival or another. Perhaps Hawking could not have had one kind of stubbornness without the other kind.

A Parting of the Ways

In the summer of 1990 shocking headlines erupted in major newspapers. Stephen and Jane Hawking were separating after almost twenty-five years of marriage. People who had seen documentaries about Hawking wondered what had become of the devoted couple whose relationship had seemed to defy death itself. Tabloid newspaper reporters began to swarm around the Hawkings, looking for sensational details about their lives, while colleagues and friends did their best to discourage the snoopers.

Gravity 1, Hawking 0

Stephen Hawking has suffered several accidents while driving his electric wheelchair. Hawking's assistant Don Page recounts one of them in A Reader's Companion. *As with the other accidents, Hawking was not seriously injured:*

"One year the Hawkings took me along when they went to a cottage in Wales, near the river Wye. This cottage was up a hill, and there was a bit of paved sidewalk that went to it. Of course, I wanted to do it in the least number of trips so I put extra batteries under [Hawking's] chair. Stephen, however, didn't realize that I'd put them under there, so he didn't know that his wheelchair was as heavily laden as possible.

So he started up this slope and got quite a bit ahead of me, about ten meters, and then he turned the corner to go into the house—but this was on the slope. I looked up and I noticed Stephen's wheelchair was slowly tipping backward. I tried to run up, but I wasn't able to move nearly rapidly enough to stop him from toppling over backward into the bushes.

It was a bit of a shocking sight to see this master of gravity overcome by the weak gravitational force of earth."

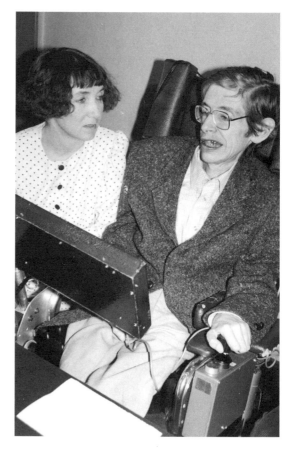

In 1990, Stephen and Jane (below) separated after twenty-five years of marriage. Despite his personal problems, Hawking continued his quest to understand the universe.

In reality, Stephen and Jane had been growing apart for a number of years. For one thing, Stephen's indifferent if not hostile attitude toward religion had clashed painfully with Jane's strong religious faith. Jane had also suffered for many long years the frustration of having to care for someone who was physically helpless, combined with almost single-handedly raising three children. Honors and adulation were showered on Stephen, but she was ignored for the most part.

As Stephen's money problems decreased, he was able to hire full-time nurses. Jane no longer had to care for him. This may have been a relief, but perhaps it also weakened the bond between them. Increasingly Stephen traveled without Jane, and Jane and the growing children became more involved with their own lives and interests. Perhaps the parting of the ways was unavoidable, but it was nonetheless painful for all concerned.

Superstardom and personal problems overshadowed Hawking's scientific work

Close Encounters of the Hollywood Kind

The movie version of Hawking's A Brief History of Time *owes much to movie producer Steven Spielberg's interest in the project. Writers Michael White and John Gribbin in their book* Stephen Hawking *recount how Spielberg became involved with Hawking's work:*

"Spielberg had been following Hawking's work for many years and, with an eye on the commercial worth of the project, was immediately interested in the idea of helping to increase public awareness of what Hawking was trying to say in *A Brief History of Time*. Spielberg is another of those who sees Hawking as the late twentieth century's answer to Albert Einstein, and has felt a deep fascination with things extraterrestrial from a very early age. . . .

Spielberg and Hawking actually met early in 1990 on the Universal lot at Amblin Studios in Los Angeles, where they posed together for photographers and chatted for over ninety minutes in the California sunshine. Expressing a mutual admiration, they apparently got on very well. Hawking had enjoyed *E.T.* and *Close Encounters of the Third Kind*. He even suggested jokingly that their film should be called *Back to the Future 4*. For his part, Spielberg had been greatly taken by *A Brief History of Time*."

Movie producer Steven Spielberg helped increase public awareness about Hawking's message in the movie version of A Brief History of Time.

for a while, but they did not bring it to an end. As the 1990s began, Hawking continued to play a part in the finding of a "theory of everything" that might explain how the forces we find in the universe today had arisen, and how they might be covered by a single, comprehensive explanation.

7 Hawking, Physics, and the Future

In 1980 an audience sat in a Cambridge auditorium to listen to the inaugural lecture of Stephen Hawking, newly appointed Lucasian Professor of Mathematics. Perhaps they were expecting a quiet summary of recent developments in physics. If so, they got a surprise. From his very first sentence, it became clear that Hawking was making waves again. He made a bold and controversial prediction:

> In this lecture I want to discuss the possibility that the goal of theoretical physics might be achieved in the not-too-distant future, say by the end of the century. By this, I mean that we might have a complete, consistent, and unified theory of the physical interactions which would describe all possible observations.[54]

A Spiral Dance Toward Understanding

Is Hawking's optimism about the forging of a "complete, consistent, and unified theory" justified? Perhaps the first step toward considering this question is to look briefly at where physics is today, and how it got there. The history of physics seems to be a kind of spiral dance in which two not quite satisfactory theories, whirling about a seeming contradiction, give birth to a more comprehensive theory. The dancers build their energy as they struggle to define their movements. Suddenly, there is a kind of flurry and their whirling movement grows wider, drawing together what has gone before and embracing new possibilities. This spiral to new understanding has already happened several times in the history of physics.

Nineteenth-century physics used two major theories to account for the phenomena of matter and energy known at the time: Newton's mechanics and James Clerk Maxwell's theories of electromagnetism. Newton's mechanics were made up of laws of gravity and motion that made it possible to predict accurately the interaction of moving bodies, such as planets orbiting the sun. Maxwell's electromagnetic equations explained how different forms of radiation, such as light and electricity, behaved.

Each of these theories worked well within its own realm. They contradicted each other, however, in trying to describe certain properties of light. Newton's law said that the speed of light should depend on the motion of the person observing it. Maxwell's equations, on the other hand, required that the speed of light be the

Nineteenth-century physics used the theories of Isaac Newton (left) and James Clerk Maxwell (right) to explain matter and energy. In some ways, however, Newton's mechanics and Maxwell's electromagnetic equations contradicted each other.

same for all observers, whether standing here on earth or speeding in a spaceship at one hundred thousand miles a second.

Near the beginning of the twentieth century Albert Einstein found a way to resolve the contradiction between Newton's and Maxwell's descriptions of light. In Einstein's theory of relativity, the speed of light was indeed fixed, but the observer's relationship to it changed. (Put another way, each observer had a different and equally valid frame of reference.) Gravity became not so much a force, as Newton had viewed it, but the way space was bent by matter so that objects were pulled toward one another.

Einstein's theories might have sounded strange to someone who had studied Newton's laws of motion. Still, the laws devised by Newton, Maxwell, and Einstein had something in common: they were precise and continuous. If you plugged values of mass, velocity, and so on into the equations of any of these systems, you could, at least in theory, get a precise answer. Also, in all these systems, quantities such as mass and energy were continuous; you

could have as much or as little of them as would fit the equations.

But light continued to make trouble for physicists, since it seemed to behave as a particle under some circumstances and as a wave under others. Starting in the 1920s, quantum physics dealt with this contradiction by drawing a picture that not only *looked* different from those of Newton, Einstein, and Maxwell, but also *worked* differently. Where the classical theories of the earlier physicists had promised precision, the quantum theories required uncertainty. An object had not a single state—position and velocity—but a range of possible states. And while the results measured by the older equations were continuous, those given by quantum theory were discrete. There were certain minimum chunks of time or distance beyond which nothing could be measured. Unlike the orbit of a planet, the path of an electron could not be anywhere that gravity decreed. Rather, the electron would take a quantum jump from one path to another if energy were added to or removed from it.

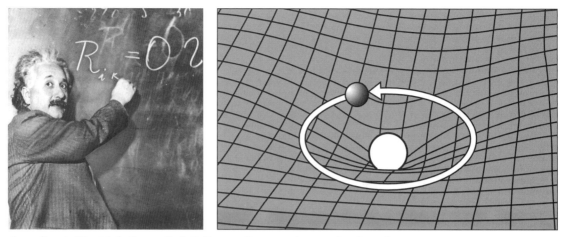

According to Einstein's theory of relativity, gravity was not so much a force, but the way space was bent by matter. The illustration at right depicts space as an infinite elastic net. Within the universe, every object with mass sinks into this net and makes a depression, which we experience as gravity. Today, Hawking searches for a "theory of everything" that will explain all the forces, including gravity, in our universe.

Just as Newton's and Maxwell's theories had been useful but limited to different areas of application, relativity and quantum mechanics—their successors—also applied to different areas. Relativity applied to the large scale of space and time, while quantum theory related to the interactions of tiny particles within atoms. As the spiral dance continued, the new theories seemed to stand wide apart.

Starting in the 1960s Stephen Hawking had found himself with a problem—the singularity and black holes—that could not be pursued beyond a certain point through relativity alone. Hawking therefore had to find a way to apply both relativity and quantum mechanics to the same problem. His success in doing so was a major achievement in modern physics. While Hawking could not unify the two theories as a whole, his work suggested ways that they could be related by viewing them against the same background: the world inside a black hole.

It gives a taste of what a unified picture of the universe might look like.

Unification of Forces

The question of unification applies not only to theories, but also to the elementary forces of the universe themselves. Any theory of everything must be able to account for four forces. Two of these forces were known in the nineteenth century. One is gravity, which causes bodies of matter to attract one another. The other is the electromagnetic force, which causes objects with opposite electrical charges (plus and minus) to attract one another and objects with the same charge to push apart.

Discoveries about the inner workings of the atom in the first part of the twentieth century revealed two additional forces. The strong nuclear force holds the particles in the nucleus of an atom (protons and neutrons) together. The weak nuclear force is responsible for radioactivity: the breakdown of atoms into other atoms or particles, yielding energy.

By the 1960s physicists were well on their way to coming up with a single theory that would explain both the electromagnetic and weak nuclear forces. This "electroweak" theory was finally confirmed in 1983 when a powerful accelerator at CERN created particles that the theory had predicted.

Meanwhile, the search for the secret of the strong force led to the discovery that such particles as protons and neutrons, once thought to be the basic building blocks of atoms, were actually made up of other particles called quarks. Physicists whimsically attached attributes such as color and charm to these particles. They tried to work out a scheme that would explain how combinations of quarks could interact to create other particles found inside atoms. Physicists today are searching for a theory that could unite the electroweak theory with the understanding of quarks and the strong nuclear force. Such a theory is called a grand unified theory, or GUT for short. Several versions of a GUT have been proposed, but none of them has become established in the way that the electroweak theory has. Furthermore, even if a satisfactory GUT were

A Contrary View

Nobel Prize-winning quantum physicist Richard Feynman did not share Hawking's optimism about the search for a theory of everything. Science writer James Gleick's biography of Feynman recounts Feynman's skepticism:

"People say to me, 'Are you looking for the ultimate laws of physics?' No, I'm not. . . . If it turns out there is an ultimate law which explains everything, so be it—it would be very nice to discover. If it turns out it's like an onion with millions of layers . . . then that's the way it is. . . . I've had a lifetime of people who believe that the answer is just around the corner. But again and again it's been a failure. Eddington, who thought that with the theory of electrons and quantum mechanics everything was going to be simple. . . . Einstein, who thought that he had a unified theory just around the corner but didn't know anything about [atomic] nuclei and was unable of course to guess it. . . . People think they're very close to the answer, but I don't think so. . . .

Whether or not nature has an ultimate, simple, unified, beautiful form is an open question, and I don't want to say either way."

devised, such a theory would still have to be expanded to account for the fourth force, gravity. Only then could it become a true theory of everything.

The Mystery of Gravity

In one sense gravity is simple: everyone knows intuitively how it works, if not why. Newton's laws give a satisfactory way to calculate the effects of gravity under ordinary circumstances. They are precise enough to plot the paths of space probes. Einstein's refinements take over at speeds near that of light. But while the other three forces can be thought of in terms of particles and broken down into discrete units called "quanta," it is not obvious how to do this with gravity. Some physicists have tried to describe a theoretical particle called a graviton that would fit into a quantum theory of gravity. Others have tried to detect gravity waves. No conclusive evidence for gravity particles or gravity waves has yet been found.

At the time Hawking gave his inaugural Lucasian lecture, the leading theory of quantum gravity was called supergravity. Hawking expressed considerable enthusiasm about this theory, claiming that it was a major step on the way to a theory of everything. But supergravity got bogged down when it turned out to require more than 150 different particles in order to work. Hawking notes that an accurate calculation to account for all of these particles would take several years with a big computer, and it still might come out wrong. When a theory turns out to be so unwieldy, it's usually a good bet that nature has something simpler in mind.

The approach to a unified theory of gravity that currently seems to be most promising is called string theory. Hawking explains:

> In string theories, what were previously thought of as particles are now pictured as waves traveling down the string, like waves on a vibrating kite string. The emission or absorption of one particle by another corresponds to the dividing or joining together of strings.[55]

In string theory, what had been considered to be a discrete particle becomes a tiny, stringlike path through space and time. The possible paths for a particle as required by the uncertainty principle can be represented as a kind of sheet of fabric woven together from these strings.

In *A Brief History of Time*, published in 1988, Hawking displayed the same kind of enthusiasm for strings as he had for supergravity in 1980. The latest version of string theory, dubbed superstring theory, seems to give a better description of quantum gravity than the earlier theories. Making connections between the mathematics of the new theory and the real physical world remains difficult, however. Equally difficult is the gathering of experimental evidence for theories that describe tiny objects that are believed to exist in as many as twenty-six dimensions!

Is the End Really Near?

Returning to Hawking's original 1980 prediction, we can ask: how near is physics to a theory of everything that can explain all the forces and interactions involved in our universe? Hawking himself admitted in his lecture that

> one has to be very cautious about making such predictions: We have thought that we were on the brink of the final synthesis [a theory to explain everything in the universe] at least twice before. At the beginning of the century it was believed that everything could be understood in terms of

---

The Terror and Beauty of Science

In A Reader's Companion *John Wheeler describes the awe and sense of responsibility that the twentieth century has brought to science. He suggests that wherever our theories might take us, the adventure of science is only beginning:*

"The first time man brought down a star to earth was five-thirty in the morning of a July day, over the New Mexico desert. And that first bit of matter, in 1945, performed according to the expectations and gave us marvelous evidence that we know how to predict, evidence that our theories are correct.

Here was something out of all experience of man on earth; and yet one could also say that the expansion of the universe, as predicted by Einstein, is so preposterous that in the beginning he couldn't believe it himself. It's the greatest evidence that man has ever been granted that our theories work and predict with a power beyond our original realization. We've had wrong theories, and the wonderful thing about the scientific community is that a wrong theory gets caught, and by finding out where it's wrong, we learn something new.

So, to me, the world around us is filled with what the old Romans used to call *flammanti moenia mundi*—the flaming ramparts of the world—the frontiers of human knowledge, all the way from how genes work, how life multiplies, how the universe expands, how black holes sop up information—all these things are frontiers not just of science, but of mankind itself. We are, in my view, just children at present. There's so much unexplored, so much marvelous, yet to be opened up. And I think, more and more, men, women, and children are coming to realize that we're embarked on mankind's most wonderful adventure today, in the here and the now, exploring these frontiers."

Hawking predicts that the space telescope could give scientists an unprecedented look into space and provide evidence for unified theories.

continuum [continuous and precise] mechanics. . . . This hope was shattered by the discovery of atomic structure and quantum mechanics. Again, in the late 1920s Max Born told a group of scientists visiting Göttingen [Germany] that "physics, as we know it, will be over in six months." This was shortly after the discovery by Paul Dirac, a previous holder of the Lucasian Chair, of the Dirac equation, which governs the behavior of the electron.[56]

One difficulty in proving or disproving possible theories of everything is that the amount of energy needed to create conditions under which they can be tested experimentally is higher than that produced in any particle accelerator we are likely to be able to build. But Hawking, a cosmologist as well as a physicist, reminds us that the farther we look into space, the earlier we see into time. As time moves back to the first tiny fraction of a second following the Big Bang, the level of energy rises to a point where the forces we see as being separate merge into one another. Perhaps the farthest, most ancient part of the universe can serve as a natural particle accelerator that can provide evidence for unified theories. Along the way we should also be able to learn whether the universe is open (forever expanding) or has enough matter to be closed by gravity toward an eventual Big Crunch.

In the early 1980s Hawking predicted:

The space telescope should allow us to determine definitely which side of the borderline the universe is on. We'll be able to look much deeper into space and get a more accurate accounting of matter in the universe.[57]

The space telescope at first suffered from delays and design errors that limited its usefulness, but it was repaired by space-walking astronauts in late 1993. The jury is still out on Hawking's bold prediction of an end to physics in the near future. As we move toward the mid-1990s, however, it does not seem likely that a true theory of everything is just around the corner. Even Hawking is careful to speak of *if* we discover such a theory, not *when*.

Hawking's Place in Science

What has the work of Stephen Hawking added to the exciting adventure of twentieth-century science? Hawking's key discoveries about singularities, black holes, and the Big Bang did more than explain puzzling cosmic phenomena. By bringing together the very different worlds of relativity and quantum mechanics, Hawking created a new way to look at the shape of space and time and the history and possible future of the universe. He also did valuable work in making the discoveries of the new physics accessible to a wide range of readers.

The fact that these achievements came despite a crippling disease that would have devastated most people has made Hawking a genuine hero and role model, not only for disabled people, but also for

Stephen Hawking—the most brilliant scientific mind of our time?

the striver in each of us. Whatever else he may yet achieve, Stephen Hawking has already advanced the spiral dance of human understanding. The drama moves toward its next act. Ahead, Hawking sees the goal and beckons us to it:

> If we do discover a complete theory, it should in time be understandable in broad principle by everyone, not just a few scientists. Then we shall all, philosophers, scientists, and just ordinary people, be able to take part in the discussion of the question of why it is that we and the universe exist. If we find the answer to that, it would be the ultimate triumph of human reason—for then we would know the mind of God.[58]

Notes

Chapter 1: An Unexpected Universe

1. Stephen Hawking, ed., *A Brief History of Time: A Reader's Companion*. New York: Bantam, 1992.

2. Hawking, ed., *A Reader's Companion*.

3. Hawking, ed., *A Reader's Companion*.

4. Hawking, ed., *A Reader's Companion*.

5. Michael White and John Gribbin, *Stephen Hawking: A Life in Science*. New York: Dutton, 1992.

6. Hawking, ed., *A Reader's Companion*.

7. White and Gribbin, *Stephen Hawking*.

8. S.W. Hawking, *A Short History* (privately produced pamphlet, cited in White and Gribbin, *Stephen Hawking*).

9. Hawking, ed., *A Reader's Companion*.

10. Hawking, ed., *A Reader's Companion*.

Chapter 2: Journey into Darkness

11. S.W. Hawking, *My Experience with ALS*, quoted in White and Gribbin, *Stephen Hawking*.

12. Hawking, ed., *A Reader's Companion*.

13. Hawking, *My Experience with ALS*, in White and Gribbin, *Stephen Hawking*.

14. Tony Osman, "A Master of the Universe," *Sunday Times Magazine*, June 19, 1988.

15. Kitty Ferguson, *Stephen Hawking: Quest for a Theory of Everything*. New York: Bantam, 1992.

16. White and Gribbin, *Stephen Hawking*.

17. White and Gribbin, *Stephen Hawking*.

18. Hawking, *A Short History*, in White and Gribbin, *Stephen Hawking*.

19. S.W. Hawking, Doctoral thesis, quoted in Ferguson, *Stephen Hawking*.

Chapter 3: Inside a Black Hole

20. Hawking, *A Short History*, in White and Gribbin, *Stephen Hawking*.

21. John Boslough, *Stephen Hawking's Universe*. New York: William Morrow and Company, Inc., 1985.

22. Bryan Appleyard, "Master of the Universe," quoted in Ferguson, *Stephen Hawking*.

23. ABC "20/20" broadcast, 1989, cited in Ferguson, *Stephen Hawking*.

24. White and Gribbin, *Stephen Hawking*.

25. Hawking, ed., *A Reader's Companion*.

26. Ian Ridpath, "Black Hole Explorer," *New Scientist*, May 4, 1978.

27. Timothy Ferris, "Mind over Matter," *Vanity Fair*, June 1984.

28. White and Gribbin, *Stephen Hawking*.

29. White and Gribbin, *Stephen Hawking*.

Chapter 4: The Moment of Creation

30. Stephen W. Hawking, *A Brief History of Time: From the Big Bang to Black Holes*. New York: Bantam, 1990.

31. S.W. Hawking, "The Edge of Space-Time," in Paul C.W. Davies, *The New Physics*. Cambridge, England: Cambridge University Press, 1989.

32. Jerry Adler, Gerald Lubenow, Maggie Malone, "Reading God's Mind," *Newsweek*, June 13, 1988.

33. Hawking, *A Brief History of Time*.

34. Boslough, *Stephen Hawking's Universe*.

Chapter 5: A Brief History of Time

35. Ellen Walton, "A Brief History of Hard Times," *Guardian*, August 9, 1989.

36. White and Gribbin, *Stephen Hawking*.

37. White and Gribbin, *Stephen Hawking*.

38. "Book News," *Bookseller*, October 21, 1988.

39. *Bookseller*, October 21, 1988.

40. Stephen W. Hawking, "A Brief History of *A Brief History*," *Popular Science*, August 1989.

41. Hawking, ed., *A Reader's Companion*.

42. Ferguson, *Stephen Hawking*.

43. White and Gribbin, *Stephen Hawking*.

44. Dennis Housby, *Cambridge Evening News*, August 30, 1988.

Chapter 6: Fame and Mixed Blessings

45. Alan Kersey, "Musical Tribute to Brave Professor," *Cambridge Evening News*, January 21, 1988.

46. White and Gribbin, *Stephen Hawking*.

47. Ferguson, *Stephen Hawking*.

48. Ferguson, *Stephen Hawking*.

49. Dennis Overbye, "The Wizard of Space and Time," quoted in White and Gribbin, *Stephen Hawking*.

50. Stephen Shames, "Stephen Hawking: A Thinking Kind of Hero," quoted in White and Gribbin, *Stephen Hawking*.

51. Osman, "A Master of the Universe."

52. "The Sky's No Limit in the Career of Stephen Hawking," *Western Australian*, quoted in White and Gribbin, *Stephen Hawking*.

53. ABC "20/20" broadcast and BBC broadcast, 1989.

Chapter 7: Hawking, Physics, and the Future

54. Stephen Hawking, "Is the End in Sight for Theoretical Physics?" Inaugural lecture, included as an appendix in *A Brief History of Time*.

55. Hawking, *A Brief History of Time*.

56. Hawking, "Is the End in Sight for Theoretical Physics?

57. Boslough, *Stephen Hawking's Universe*.

58. Hawking, *A Brief History of Time*.

For Further Reading

Kitty Ferguson, *Stephen Hawking: Quest for a Theory of Everything*. New York: Bantam, 1992. Focuses on Hawking's scientific work and includes diagrams that illustrate important concepts of physics.

Stephen Hawking, ed., *A Brief History of Time: A Reader's Companion*. New York: Bantam, 1992. A collection of quotes from Hawking's family, friends, and colleagues that brings out his human side.

Stephen Hawking, *A Brief History of Time: From the Big Bang to Black Holes*. New York: Bantam, 1990. This is Hawking's most complete account of his work. Not easy reading, but rewarding.

Stephen Hawking, *Black Holes and Baby Universes*. New York: Bantam, 1983. A collection of Hawking's earlier writings—essays, talks, and interviews.

Dennis Overbye, *Lonely Hearts of the Cosmos: The Story of the Scientific Quest for the Secret of the Universe*. New York: HarperCollins, 1991. This account of the lives and work of the key astronomers of our time is written in a dramatic, engaging style. It shows how astronomers have devoted their lives to answering questions about the origin and destiny of the universe.

Michael White and John Gribbin, *Stephen Hawking: A Life in Science*. New York: Dutton, 1992. A well-balanced biography that discusses Hawking's work and the events of his life in alternate chapters.

Additional Works Consulted

John Boslough, *Stephen Hawking's Universe.* New York: William Morrow and Company, Inc., 1985. Focuses mainly on Hawking's work, with just enough about his life to put things in context.

James Gleick, *Genius: The Life and Science of Richard Feynman.* New York: Pantheon, 1992. Feynman's life, like Hawking's, is full of dramatic twists and great stories. The contrast between the backgrounds and personalities of the two great physicists is also interesting.

John Gribbin, *Cosmic Coincidences: Dark Matter, Mankind, and Anthropic Cosmology.* New York: Bantam, 1989. If reading about Hawking makes you want to explore theories about the ultimate nature of the universe, this book will give you some intriguing ideas to think about.

William J. Kaufmann III, *Discovering the Universe.* New York: W.H. Freeman, 1987. A good general introduction to astronomy and astrophysics that provides useful background to Hawking's work.

Fred Alan Wolf, *Taking the Quantum Leap: The New Physics for Nonscientists.* New York: Harper & Row, 1989. A good nonmathematical introduction to the often puzzling ideas of quantum physics.

Index

Picture Credits

Cover photo © 1994 by Abe Frajndlich

AP/Wide World Photos, 18, 20, 30, 45, 52, 60, 66, 73, 76 (bottom), 80 (left), 84

Godfrey Argent/Camera Press London, 24, 47

Berry/Space Telescope Science Institute, 53

The Bettmann Archive, 49

© Chris Butler/Astrostock, 43

Camera Press London, 51

© 1994 by Abe Frajndlich, 38

Library of Congress, 13, 79 (left)

Manni Mason's Pictures, 10, 12, 15, 16 (both), 19, 34 (top), 76 (top)

NASA, 32, 56

National Archives, 11

Richard Open, Camera Press London, 65, 67

Reuters/Bettmann, 68, 70, 77

Smithsonian Institution, 14 (bottom)

Terence Spencer/Camera Press London, 62

Stock Montage/Historical Pictures, 79 (right)

Homer Sykes/Camera Press London, 9, 39, 40, 71, 72

Homer Sykes, Woodfin Camp & Associates, 85

Peter Trievnor/Camera Press London, 34 (bottom)

UPI/Bettmann, 15 (top), 22, 28, 29, 37, 48

About the Author

Harry Henderson's interest in science began at an early age when he devoured popular books by writers such as Fred Hoyle and George Gamow. He writes and edits books about computer languages and operating systems and also writes material for elementary and high school textbooks on a variety of subjects. Sometimes he collaborates with his wife, Lisa Yount, on writing projects. He and Lisa live in El Cerrito, California, surrounded by computers, books, and an indeterminate number of cats.